HOW TO GET AN EQUITY RESEARCH ANALYST JOB

A Guide to Starting a Career in Asset Management

About the Author

Gillian Elcock has worked as an equity research analyst for several years at respected asset management companies in the U.S. and the UK, including Putnam Investments and Insight Investment. She started her career as a management consultant at The Boston Consulting Group.

She holds an MBA from the Harvard Business School and MEng and BSc degrees from the Massachusetts Institute of Technology.

You can visit her blog at **www.dennyellison.com.**

HOW TO GET AN

EQUITY RESEARCH ANALYST Job

A Guide to Starting a Career in **Asset Management**

Gillian D. Elcock

How to Get an Equity Research Analyst Job

First published in 2010 by:

Ecademy Press

48 St Vincent Drive, St Albans, Herts, AL1 5SJ

info@ecademy-press.com

www.ecademy-press.com

Printed and Bound by: Lightning Source in the UK and USA

Set in Warnock Pro and Myriad by Karen Gladwell

Cover artwork and illustrations by Michael Inns

Printed on acid-free paper from managed forests. This book is printed on demand, so no copies will be remaindered or pulped.

ISBN 978-1-905823-93-2

Contents

Acknowledgements

I would like to greatly thank the reviewers of this book including Tim Codrington, Carmina Buzuloiu, Christianne Elcock, and Peter Renton. Their comments and suggestions were invaluable.

I would also like to thank Mindy Gibbins-Klein of The Book Midwife and Ecademy Press. Her guidance and coaching enabled me to write this book in a structured manner and at an impressive pace.

My parents, brother, sisters, and entire family have given me great love and support during the writing of the book and at all times. Thank you.

Preface

I have worked as a buy side equity research analyst for several years. I entered the asset management industry straight after I graduated from business school. I started my career in the U.S. and then moved to London, in the UK.

Before business school, I worked in management consulting in New York City. When I decided that I wanted to work in equity research, I found that there wasn't a lot of written help on the topic. There were many resources that dealt with investment banking roles, but not much on research specifically.

Luckily, I went to a very large Boston-based business school in the U.S., with investment clubs and helpful second-year students who guided me through the process. Many asset management companies came on campus to recruit, and that is how I got both my summer and full-time positions. However, I still think that I would have benefited from a book that explained the industry and how to prepare for interviews. This is my attempt to write such a book.

This book is targeted primarily towards students: business school students and undergraduates who would like a career in equity research, particularly in asset management i.e. on the buy side. The book should also be helpful for other people who want to get into the industry, for example those with experience in other areas of finance or in other industries altogether. However, many of the examples I use and much of the advice I give is written with students and people who are early in their careers in mind.

Though I am focused on the buy side, this book should also be helpful to people who are interested in sell-side equity research positions, because the interview processes are quite similar. During my career I have interviewed with both the buy and sell side, and received job offers from both.

That being said, I have only ever worked on the buy side. In addition, my experience has been quite specific: fundamental equity research, mostly long-only. The book will be relevant for people who want to work at hedge funds, but mainly if they want to do fundamental research (long or short). This book will be less helpful to people interested in fixed income research, quantitative research, or technical analysis roles.

It can be tough to break into asset management. It is not a big industry in its hiring relative to other branches of finance. In addition, people already on the buy side can sometimes be quite sceptical about the desire of others to enter the industry.

Luckily, I have a lot of experience that I can draw upon to guide you through the process of finding an equity research job. I have had several interviews of all different types at many asset management companies in both the U.S. and the UK (and once in Asia). I have received several job offers, and have of course been turned down for interviews and jobs many times.

This book distils all of this experience into guidelines, tips, and advice that will help you to identify the firms you might want to work for, get interviews, then prepare for and execute the interviews well. At the end of the book I even give you a few tips to start you off on the right foot in your first buy side role. I hope you can learn from my mistakes as well as my successes, as I share my experiences and lessons learnt with you.

Please note, however, that because the book is based on my experiences, almost the entire work consists of statements of my opinions on various matters. You are of course free to agree or disagree with me on any point, and do what you think is best. At the end of the day, you have to do what feels right for you. All I can hope is that you will find some of my advice useful on your journey to getting a job in equity research or asset management. I wish you the best of luck. It is a great industry to work in.

Chapter 1

Understand the Asset Management Industry, the Analyst Role, and the Differences between the Buy and Sell Side

Given that you've picked up this book, you probably have some idea about what asset management is, and what an equity research analyst does. However, I thought it would still be a good idea to describe the industry and the role. I'll also compare the buy-side and the sell-side. My descriptions of the latter will be based mainly on my observations, as I have never worked on the sell-side, only on the buy-side.

Please note that I may sometimes hyphenate the words "buy-side" and "sell-side", and at other times I may just write them as two separate words.

Explaining the Asset Management Industry or the "Buy-Side"

The asset management industry refers to a collection of companies that manage assets (money) on behalf of others. Another widely used term for the industry is investment management. In finance, these companies are also referred to as the buy side. Because the companies control assets, they can go into the capital markets and buy stocks and other securities, hence the term.

The assets that these companies manage may, for example, consist of people's retirement funds or pension plans, money being invested for the education of children, or general savings for the future. A popular way to do this nowadays, of course, is via mutual funds, and some asset management firms do offer mutual funds to the public. In some countries similar investment vehicles are called unit trusts.

The assets that these companies manage are usually held in pools called "portfolios" or "funds". In order for the investment management companies to know exactly which securities to put into their portfolios, they need people to do extensive research and analysis. When those securities are stocks (or equities), the people who do the research are called "Equity Research Analysts". The people who make the final decisions about which securities are bought and sold, and who manage the asset pools, are called "portfolio managers" or "fund managers", terms you may have heard a lot. Sometimes the roles of portfolio manager and analyst are combined in a hybrid role.

Buy-side firms can, of course, sell stocks as well as buy them. They can also short stocks, i.e. sell stocks they don't own with the aim of buying them back later at a lower price.

Asset Managers Vary in Size

There are many different types of asset management companies. They go from very large ones with tens of billions of dollars of assets under management (AUM) to small boutique firms with a few million. Some of the well-known names in the U.S. include Fidelity, Wellington, T. Rowe Price, Franklin Templeton and The Capital Group. Some of the big firms in the UK include Schroders, Threadneedle, and Newton (most of the large American firms will have offices in London as well).

But it is important to note that in addition to these big gorillas of the industry, there are hundreds of smaller firms around the world. There is a big concentration of them in the U.S. and the U.K, the two countries I have worked in. But there are firms in many other places as well. Any major financial centre is bound to have a few.

The Buy Side Includes Hedge Funds

The buy-side includes hedge funds, a group of companies that has gained a lot of attention and some notoriety over the years. Hedge funds tend to be smaller companies (in terms of assets), though there are a few giant ones out there. They also tend to be more specialized in their investment techniques than the big firms. They are usually more likely to short stocks, use leverage, or employ other strategies that may be considered riskier than traditional long-only buy-and-hold investing. Hedge funds also tend to have a different fee structure from the traditional firms, one which allows them to share some of the upside if they make money for their investors. This accounts for the very large compensation numbers that are sometimes available and often reported at hedge funds.

Important Terms: Long and Short

Two terms that are very important to understand when discussing the investment world are "long" and "short". They are different ways of saying "buy" and "sell". To go long a stock is to buy it. To short a stock is a bit more complicated than just selling it. If a fund already owns a stock it can sell it. But to short a stock means to borrow it and sell it into the market. Later, the stock will be bought back, hopefully at a lower price, and returned to the lender. Most traditional buy side firms are long-only: i.e. they will not short stocks, only buy and sell them. Shorting is often done by hedge funds, and the practice has received negative press from time to time. If a firm does short stocks it is often called "long/short" to differentiate it from "long-only" companies. For the purposes of interviewing, you need to understand that if you are asked for a short idea, it means that you need to come up with a stock that you would sell, whereas if someone asks you for a long idea, you need to present a stock that you would buy.

Asset Managers Have Different Investment Styles

Buy-side firms may have specific investment styles that they adhere to. Common examples include Value, Growth, and GARP (Growth at a Reasonable Price). They may also focus on specific geographies and/or stocks of certain market capitalizations (e.g. small-cap stocks or mid-cap stocks). Some large firms may have separate fund management groups that each focus on specific styles and geographies. So, for example, there may be a Large Cap Value team as well as a Small & Mid-Cap Value team. Or there may be a UK Growth Group. The key here is that you should be aware of these distinctions when you are interviewing with a firm or a particular group within a firm.

Value Investing: Value investors focus on buying stocks that are very cheaply valued. They usually believe that companies have an intrinsic value that can be estimated from things like their earnings, assets, and dividends. They will only buy shares if they are trading well below this intrinsic value. Value investors tend to be sceptical about paying for future earnings growth. They prefer to invest in reliable, consistent companies that have been around for a long time, and they will usually avoid the hot new start-ups. Some have an absolute level beyond which they will not pay for a company, no matter what, for example, 16x earnings. Value investors also tend to have the longest time horizons in the investment community. They are willing to buy a stock that is cheap and wait patiently until the market realizes that it is worth more. They are less concerned with near-term catalysts that will get the stock moving. Benjamin Graham is often thought of as the father of value investing, and Warren Buffett, who was one of Graham's students, is one of the world's most famous value investors.

Growth Investing: Growth investing is often positioned at the other end of the spectrum to Value. As the name implies, Growth investors are looking for companies that are likely to grow their sales and profits quickly for a sustained period. Investors of this sort are not interested in a company just because it is cheap. They are more willing to look out into the future, project what a company may earn, and pay up for some of those earnings and cash flows today. Growth investors are therefore more willing to buy companies that are trading on relatively high multiples of current earnings, and that would look expensive to a more value oriented investor. Growth investors are also trying to buy companies for less than what they are worth in the long-run. That being said, they usually have more of a focus on catalysts and what happens in the short-term. The Growth investor wants proof that the companies he or she has invested in are in fact growing quickly, beating earnings, launching new products, etc. He or she knows that if a company does not deliver on its promises of good growth, the market is likely to become disappointed, and the stock could sell-off.

GARP Investing: GARP tries to straddles the difference between the Value and Growth investment styles. It stands for "Growth at a Reasonable Price". GARP investors are interested in finding companies that have good growth prospects. However, they are also careful about valuation, and what they pay for a company. They may not require a stock to be as cheap as the Value investor, but they need to prove that its valuation is attractive or at least reasonable.

Cap Focus and Investment Time Horizon

As I mentioned previously, stocks are often also classified by the size of their market capitalization, or "market cap". The market cap of a company is the number of shares outstanding times the current stock price. There is no precise definition of what makes a company small, medium, or large, but generally, companies are considered large-cap if they are $10 billion US dollars or more in size; extremely large companies, say $100 billion and above, may be referred to as "mega caps". Companies are typically mid-cap if they are $1 billion to $10 billion in size, and small-cap if they are under $1 billion. Again, these are just guidelines. Different firms may have different cut-offs for these definitions. If a strategy is "All-Cap" it just means that companies of any size can be invested in by that fund/portfolio.

Another distinction is the time horizon of investing, which I touched on in the description of Value investing. Most traditional equity asset managers profess to have a medium-to-long-term investment horizon. That usually means anywhere from 6 months to 5 years, typically 12-18 months. What is the significance of this? It means that the company expects, on average, to hold a stock for that length of time, and to give a stock that amount of time to get working. Some companies, however, will have a much shorter time horizon, maybe just a few days, or even intra-day. This is more likely to be found at hedge funds, and is something you should be aware of when you go in for an interview.

The information in this book is written with more of a medium to long-term investment horizon in mind, however, most of it should be applicable if you are interviewing with a more short-term place. You may just need to tweak your stock pitch somewhat, and make sure you have some catalysts that you know could make the stock work in the very near-term (see Chapter 4 (II) for more information).

Don't Worry Too Much about These Distinctions

At this point you may be feeling confused, and wondering how you will ever pick which type of firm to work for. At the beginning of your career or your first job out of business school, unless you do already have a strong preference somehow, it probably doesn't matter that much. You just want to get some experience picking stocks. As time goes on, you may develop a preference for a particular investment style or capitalization group, and decide to move to a company or a group within a company that specializes in whatever you are interested in.

High Level Categories in the Asset Management Industry

There are even higher-level categories of description for investment management firms, and I am going to describe them briefly.

There are firms that are focused on equities (or stocks), on fixed income securities (bonds), and on other specialized asset classes (e.g. LDI, hybrids). There are also companies that specialize in fundamental, quantitative, or technical analysis.

Remember that an investment management firm may house many different investing types under one roof. You just need to find the right group or department for you.

> *Please note that this book is focused on helping you to acquire a job in*
> *FUNDAMENTAL EQUITY research.*

Technical analysis involves observing, tracking, and analyzing the price movement of stocks (and other securities). From patterns that are formed in stock movements over time, technical analysis attempts to predict what the stock movement is likely to be in the future. No attention is paid to the revenues, earnings, and cash flow of the companies that are associated with the stocks. The price movements themselves give the analysts all the information they need.

Quantitative analysis techniques use information about companies' historical sales, earnings, cash flow etc, as well as data about their stock price action over certain periods. This information is often aggregated in various ways to give the company a score which captures how it has performed. Companies with high scores are considered more likely to perform well in the future, so the quant investor will look to invest in the shares of these companies, as opposed to those with low scores. Quantitative analysis is very numbers driven, with priority given to hard data rather than qualitative information about a company or its management. Some quantitative analysis techniques use sophisticated mathematical models to price stocks and make trading decisions.

Fundamental analysis involves more than just looking at stock prices and historical data about a company. It also does not usually involve complicated mathematical models. Fundamental analysts attempt to figure out what a company is worth by understanding the drivers of that company's performance. Even here, there is a distinction between "top-down" and "bottom-up" fundamental analysis. Top-down analysis looks at factors like interest rates, GDP growth rates, exchange rates, and other macro-economic drivers that may affect an industry. If the trends are supportive of that industry, then stocks within it are deemed attractive, provided they meet certain criteria.

This Book Deals with Bottoms-Up Fundamental Analysis

This book deals with "bottoms-up" fundamental analysis. The works starts with the company itself, and the analyst attempts to understand the industry the company operates in, how the company is positioned, its products and services, and the competency of its management team. The analyst often builds a model to forecast the earnings of the company, and to determine what the company is worth. This will be a key determinant of whether the stock is bought or sold. However, both qualitative and quantitative factors will considered when making this decision.

Explaining the Sell-Side

Even though the focus of this book is on getting a buy-side job, there are quite a few similarities between the roles of buy-side and sell-side analysts, as well as some key differences. It is not unusual for people to switch between the buy and sell-side. Therefore, I am going to spend a bit of time describing the sell-side in this chapter. It may be the case that, during your quest to work on the buy-side, you choose to work on the sell-side for a summer or for a short period after you graduate. Many of the interview techniques discussed later in this book are applicable to the sell-side as well.

The sell-side refers to companies that market research, typically to the buy-side. They are, effectively, "selling" their research, hence the term. They don't manage money or control assets like the buy-side does.

Sell-side analysts tend to publish their research. So when you hear on the news or CNBC that an analyst has upgraded or downgraded a stock, this will be coming from the sell-side, not the buy-side. Buy-side analysts do not usually publish their research to anyone outside of the company they work for or even to specific people within that company.

Sell-side analysts are usually found at investment banks (like Goldman Sachs, Morgan Stanley, Merrill Lynch, etc). There are also other smaller brokerage firms and independent organizations that market their research.

The role of the sell-side analyst has attracted some controversy in recent years, especially after the dot-com crash of 2000. Some analysts were accused of publishing biased, too-positive research on the dot-com companies in order to generate revenue for the investment banking arms of their companies. After this fall-out, many regulations were introduced to address these issues. This is not the focus of this book, but it is something you should be aware of and potentially do more research on if you are considering working on the sell-side.

What's Coming Next

Now that I have given you an overview of what buy-side and sell-side companies do, I am going to describe the roles of the buy-side equity research analyst and the sell-side equity research analyst in some detail. I will also touch on what a fund manager does. My assumption is that you want to become an analyst. Even if you eventually want to become a fund manager, it is very likely that the first step on that path will be performing the duties of an analyst, even if you are called by another name (like "trainee fund manager").

The Role of Buy-Side Equity Research Analyst

Your main job as a buy-side analyst is to come up with buy/sell recommendations for stocks. The simplest way to describe your job is this: you are a stock-picker. However, there tends to be a lot of infrastructure placed around this simple concept.

The Coverage List

Usually, when you join a company, you will be given a list of stocks that you are expected to "cover" or "follow". Simply put, these are the companies that you are expected to come up with buy or sell recommendations for. They will become your companies "under coverage". The list will usually be comprised of companies in a certain sector or sub-sector, and in a particular geography. Examples include "US Industrials" or "European Banks". Sometimes you may be given more than one sector/geography to cover, but usually not more than three. Some roles might require you to cover companies in all geographies, e.g. "Global Oil & Gas". The bigger the firm you are at, and the larger the research pool of analysts, the smaller your coverage list is likely to be. At a very small firm with not many analysts, you are likely to be given more sectors and more stocks.

Note that when you join a company at the start of your career, you are unlikely to be given much choice in what sector you can cover. For instance, I was assigned a subset of the North American and European industrials on my first job. Did I have a particular interest in industrials? No, none at all, but they needed someone to cover the sector. Nevertheless, it had quite a big impact on my career, because I continued to cover the sector for several years afterwards. My second job was a position that specifically required an experienced Industrials Analyst.

It is possible to switch sectors, however, so don't get too hung up on what you get at first. Some employers just want a good stock-picker, and realize that the skill is transferable from one sector to another, and from one geography to another.

Now that you have your coverage list, your first task will be to understand the industry or industries the companies are in, what the companies do, and how they make money. You then have to do detailed research on each company to investigate and understand its strategy, financials, and management.

Working with Management and the Sell-Side

To aid them in this process, most buy-side analysts will work with the sell-side. They will read sell-side research, and maybe call or meet with the analysts who cover the same sectors or stocks.

Analysts also interact with the management teams of the companies they cover. For large companies, a typical point of contact is someone in the Investor Relations division. This area of the company is specifically set up to give information to investors and to address their concerns. Smaller companies may assign this function to the Controller or someone else in management. Analysts also periodically meet with the senior management of their companies under coverage: typically the CEO and/or CFO. This may happen when the company visits the asset management firm, or when the analyst attends conferences. The analyst is expected to prepare questions and interview the management.

Analysts often try to learn more about their industries by speaking not just with the companies they cover, but with other participants in the value chain. So they may try to establish relationships with suppliers and customers of their companies under coverage as well. They may keep track of published industry data about all of these industries, to keep abreast of trends and inflexion points.

Valuation is a Key Job of the Analyst

An extremely important part of the work of the buy-side analyst is valuation. This is where you decide how much a stock is worth. There are whole books written on this subject alone, and you have probably done some valuation work in your finance courses. There are several valuation methods and metrics, including DCF (discounted cash flow), P/E, P/B, P/S, dividend yield, DDM, etc. The good news is that you will usually not be totally left alone on this. Most investment management research departments and fund management groups have strong preferences about which valuation methodologies they like to use, and you will learn what those are when you arrive on the job.

Note that most valuation methodologies require you to build a model that forecasts the financial performance of each company for a few years. Some asset managers are more heavily into modelling than others. Some buy-side analysts like to start with models they get from the sell-side and then build in their own assumptions. Either way, the financial and valuation model you build and maintain for each company in your coverage list is likely to become a key part of your work. So if you hate finance, Excel, and number crunching, this job is likely not one for you. But you probably already know that.

Coming up with a Recommendation

The next step is the most important one: you put all of the pieces together: i.e. your view of the industry, your view of a company's products, financial performance, management, and valuation, as well as other factors like the market's and sell-side's perceptions of the stock, and you decide on a rating for the stock. Some places may call this a "grade" or "recommendation".

A rating is a buy, sell, or hold recommendation. You may find various incarnations of this at your company. Some may have "Strong Buy" and "Buy" (and the matching sells); others may have "Outperform" and "Buy" (Buy is a stronger signal than Outperform). Some companies will not have a "Hold" rating. Others may use numbers where 1=Strong Buy and 4= Strong Sell. But whatever the terminology, the key is you have to decide what you think about each stock.

Analysts Have to Present their Research and Keep Track of Stocks

Finally, buy-side analysts are usually required to present their recommendations in some form. All your brilliant analysis and research is not worth much if no one reads it. Portfolio managers (PMs) are the main users of buy-side research. If there is a Director of Research, he or she will probably want to read your research as well. You may have to publish your work to a central database within your company, or you may just be expected to present your findings orally. Either way, convincing the PMs to take his/her research seriously and follow the recommendations within it is a key part of any buy-side analyst's job.

Analysts are also expected to keep track of the performance of their companies, including earnings results, and the stock price. If something important happens to a company, or the stock price moves significantly, or sometimes even if a sell-side analyst upgrades or downgrades the stock, the analyst is expected to make a comment or recommend action (if appropriate). If the analyst decides to change a rating (e.g. Buy goes to Hold), he/she is expected to let the fund managers know right away, because they may want to take some action based on the change in recommendation.

The Fund Managers Have the Final Decision

This brings me to another key point about the buy-side analyst role. When you make a recommendation on a stock, the fund managers have a choice as to whether or not they follow that recommendation. Ultimately, your use as an analyst will be measured, at least to some extent, by how much they do follow you. So part of your job is getting the PMs (portfolio managers) to trust you as an analyst.

As with everything else, some firms emphasize this more than others. At some asset managers, analysts may be judged mainly by how well their recommendations actually do, with little thought as to whether or not anyone actually follows them. But I think this is rare. Most firms will try to make sure the analysts interact with the PMs and try to get their ideas into the funds. They usually do this by structuring their incentive plans accordingly. This can be a touchy subject for some analysts, who may complain that stubborn, arrogant PMs will refuse to follow their advice no matter what they do. But the reality is that it is part of the buy-side analyst's job to get the fund managers to listen to and act on their stock recommendations. In this sense, buy-side analysts do have to do a bit of "selling" as well.

Undergrad versus MBA Student – Your Role Will Be Different

Please note that your initial duties as an analyst are likely to vary depending on whether you are entering the industry out of university or out of business school. Business school graduates are likely to be given their own stocks to cover right away, and expected to perform the duties I have described above. University graduates are often initially assigned to work with a senior analyst for some time to learn the ropes. The thought here is that undergrads usually do not have the training or know-how to cover stocks on their own right away. If they show that they are capable, university grads may eventually be given their own stocks. Some asset management companies may require recent graduates to go to business school after 2-3 years, while others may allow them to be promoted to the MBA-level position. The MBA tends to be more valued in the U.S., so this practice is more likely to be found there, or at companies based in the U.S. People are more likely to be allowed to work their way up in the UK, without an MBA. However, many UK firms value the CFA[1] designation, and may even require graduates to obtain it while they are working at the company.

The situation is a bit trickier for people who have other graduate degrees, e.g. people who have been to law or medical school, or have masters or PhDs in other subjects, and not an MBA or another business-related degree. Each asset manager will have its own policy about at which level these people will enter the firm, assuming they do hire from this pool of students.

Research is either Centralized or Decentralized

There are two main models of how analysts are allocated within an asset management firm: centralized research or decentralized within a portfolio group.

Larger companies are more likely to have a centralized model. Analysts become part of the research organization and will often report to a Director of Research. They are then expected to build relationships with the various portfolio management teams within the firm and present their stock ideas to them.

In the decentralized model, analysts are assigned to work with a specific group of fund managers (e.g. the Large Cap Value team). They work only on the funds associated with that group and target their ideas towards an investment style that would be appropriate for them. The analyst will then usually report to the head of that investment team, typically a portfolio manager.

Some firms operate a matrix system in which an analyst is a member of both a portfolio group and a research team.

---

[1] CFA stands for Chartered Financial Analyst. The CFA Charter is earned by passing 3 exams.

The Role of Fund Manager/Portfolio Manager

The fund manager or portfolio manager role is the other key one on the buy-side. Very simply, fund managers work with analysts, as I have described above, and make the final decisions on whether or not, when, and how much to buy and sell each stock. In some firms, there is a well-defined portfolio manager track, where you start off as an analyst, and then can become a fund manager over time. At other firms, you are expected to become a "career analyst", i.e. it is not expected or desired for you to ever become a portfolio manager. If you are interested in becoming a PM, you should know the policy of the firm you are going to work for before you join it.

The Role of Sell-Side Equity Research Analyst

The sell-side analyst role has many similarities to the buy-side analyst one, so please read that section, as here I will be highlighting the differences.

As I've mentioned previously, it is not uncommon for people to switch between the buy and sell side. So if you do want to work on the buy-side, it might be worth interviewing on the sell-side as well.

The Sell Side Markets to the Buy Side

One of the main roles of the sell-side analyst is to get buy-side analysts and fund managers to value their research. Sell-side analysts may interact with fund managers, but their primary relationship is usually with the buy-side analyst. The buy-side expresses its value for sell-side research through "voting" for each analyst. This is a rather complicated process which I won't go into here, but suffice it to say that there is a way for the buy-side to periodically express how much they value the research they are getting, and that this is very important to the sell-side.

The Sell Side Tends to Cover Fewer Stocks

As it is done on the buy-side, a sell-side analyst will have a list of stocks or "names" that he or she is expected to cover, usually grouped by sector and geography. However, each sell-side analyst tends to focus on a smaller number of names than her buy side counterpart. This is because sell-side analysts are generally expected to know their stocks in a great deal of depth, and have very detailed quarterly or semi-annual and annual models for each company, that are constantly updated. Analysts tend to be in constant touch with the management of the companies they follow, and they publish notes often, usually at least once per quarter, when the company reports its earnings (or once every 6 months if the company reports semi-annually). In addition, when they initiate on a company, sell-side analysts are usually expected to write a very long, in-depth note, with a great deal of industry and company background information. They may also periodically write long industry thought-pieces or short company update notes. As mentioned previously, the sell-side publishes their research. This research will go to their clients on the buy-side and may go to the press and other observers, so it has to be of a very high, professional standard. Because they have to do so much work for each stock, the sell-side can only cover so many.

It is also not uncommon, especially at the big investment banks, to find a team of analysts covering a sector. There is usually a lead analyst, the primary "name" on the stock, who will have a few junior analysts who provide analytical and client support. If you are hired right out of business school or undergrad to the sell-side, you are likely to first work as a junior analyst.

Positive Bias in Sell Side Research?

Sell-side analysts also give buy, sell, and hold recommendations. However, there tends to be more of a bias towards positive (buy) recommendations. The industry has come under criticism for this in the past and may continue to do so in the future. But it is quite hard to be negative on the sell-side. In particular, the management of the companies under recommendation tend not to like it when their stocks are rated "Sell". And part of the sell-side analyst's job is to have a good relationship with the companies' management and investor relations teams.

Now, none of this is a secret in the industry. In particular, the buy-side knows very well that sell-side research tends to maybe be a bit more positive than it should. Therefore, it tends not to be considered as important on the sell-side as it is on the buy-side to get the actual recommendation right. People will pay attention to the ratings, and to changes in the ratings, yes, especially if they move a stock. But the buy-side usually values the sell-side for many things other than the actual buy/sell stock ratings.

There Are Many Ways to Add Value on the Sell Side

And that brings us to another key point about being a sell-side analyst: there are many ways to add value to your clients. You can be really good at writing industry notes that give a lot of background information on a particular sector; you can get to know management teams really well; you can do unique periodic surveys of a certain customer base; you can put on great conferences or organize trips to visit hard-to-see companies. These are just some of the ways a sell-side analyst can differentiate herself from the pack. It's not just about whether you have a buy or a sell on a particular company. Your buy-side clients may not pay much attention to that anyway – they think that coming up with the right recommendation on a stock is their job, not yours.

Contrast this with the buy-side where your main job (and the driver of your compensation) is to get the stock picks right. I hope you are beginning to see some of the differences between the buy and sell side.

The Sell Side Analyst Role Can Be High Profile

The sell-side role can be a very high-profile one. A sell-side analyst is building up a franchise that is based largely around himself or herself. When a powerful analyst changes a recommendation on a stock, it can move the stock price (for a day or two, at least), and make the (financial) news.

Sell Side Analysts Tend to Work Longer Hours

Sell-side analysts have to market their research to many more constituents than a buy-side analyst does, and they often spend a fair amount of time travelling to meet clients and companies. The job involves presenting their work to many people. In addition to working directly with the buy side, sell-side analysts often also have to do some internal marketing with their company's institutional sales force to get them to value and push their research. This is because the salespeople can sometimes be very influential in helping the analyst to get in front of the buy side. Because of all of this, plus the large amount of writing required for the job, the hours on the sell-side tend to be much longer than they are on the buy-side.

Buy Side or Sell Side: Which One is Better for You?

So is the sell-side for you? Well my impression is that the sell-side is better for relatively outgoing people who can handle well or even enjoy the talking, presenting, and marketing aspects of the role, as well as the research and analysis. It's okay to be a bit quirky and nerdy on the buy-side, as long as you get the stocks right. Not so on the sell-side, it seems to me.

However, the marketing and selling aspects become more important as you become more senior on the sell-side. Initially, if you join a sell-side team, your focus is likely to be on learning how to research and value stocks. And these are the key similarities to the role on the buy-side.

Why Work in the Industry?

I've described the key roles in the asset management industry, and maybe they (still) seem very interesting to you. But you may be wondering about the bigger picture - things like whether the industry is a good one to join, what its long-term prospects are, and whether it adds any value to society.

Favourable Trends

In my view, the long-term outlook for the industry is quite favourable. Asset management is a very profitable business, with high margins and returns, and there has always been a real demand from investors for expertise in how their money is managed. There has been talk of fees in the industry coming under pressure and there is always some risk of that. However the outlook for demand seems favourable. As many of the large emerging economies continue to develop and industrialize, their need for investment management services is likely to grow. The expanding populations in many developing countries are likely to drive demand in future years. And in many developed countries, aging populations and longer life spans mean that wealth and asset management services are going to be increasingly vital, as people need to ensure that they have enough saved up to last them through their retirement years.

Work Life Balance and Objective Measurement

Working in asset management has many advantages. In addition to being an exciting and potentially lucrative career, there is generally a better work-life balance than can be found in some other branches of finance. Hours tend to revolve around those of the market, so they are not overly long. Performance can be measured objectively and concretely, and is not left up to whether or not the boss likes the way you dress: if your stocks picks did well, so did you.

But Scale Economics Mean Fewer Jobs

Because of these positive characteristics, buy side jobs tend to be in high demand. However, the industry does not need as many people as some other areas of finance. This is partly because there are large scale economies in the business. One fund manager and a few analysts can be hired to manage a $100 million portfolio. If they have good performance and attract additional money, that fund might grow to $500 million. But the same team can manage this bigger portfolio, they do not need to go out and hire 5 times as many people. At some of the very large asset managers, there are funds that are tens of billions of dollars in size that are being managed by one person (though he or she will be supported by the analyst pool at that firm). Because of this supply/ demand imbalance of labour, asset management jobs are quite hard to get, and the interview process is very competitive.

Your Role as an Intermediary is Important

I think it is also important to stress that equity research analyst and fund management jobs are ones that need to be taken seriously by people that enter the industry. They are not just about having fun and playing the markets. When you are an equity analyst on either the buy or sell side, you are an intermediary in the capital raising process of the global financial markets. The integrity of this process is critical, and it is something you should think carefully about. The work you do helps to put a value on publicly traded assets. This often has a trickle down impact on the values of other economic assets. In addition, asset management companies are entrusted with the hard-earned money of others, and have a fiduciary responsibility to the asset owner. As an analyst or fund manager, you are helping to invest for others: savings, pensions and retirement, education of children, etc. It's important work, and you should always think about the implications of your actions.

What Should You Study?

Though the equity research analyst role is quite a quantitative one in many respects, most asset managers and sell-side institutions are open to taking students that have degrees in almost any discipline. You will find people that have majored in languages, history, and the humanities as well as finance, business, and economics. So if you are an undergraduate student, you don't have to worry that you are studying the wrong thing. A lot of your training will be on the job. That being said, it might be useful to take a few courses in finance, accounting, or business strategy, if only to test whether you are interested in these topics at all. Obviously, business school students will have exposure to these subjects from day one. It could be helpful to take some advanced courses in these areas.

The truth is the most important requirement to a career in equity research is a genuine interest in the markets and in stocks, even if you haven't studied them formally and your major is something completely different. Therefore it will be helpful, though not absolutely necessary, if you have invested personally, or if you can demonstrate that you follow the markets and are interested in what goes on in the financial world.

What's Coming Next

Hopefully you now have a good sense of the buy-side, the sell-side, and the main duties of the equity research analyst on each side of the fence.

The next few chapters are focused on getting and doing well in interviews for equity research positions. I am focusing on the buy-side from here on, and giving advice based on my experience of getting jobs at investment management companies.

However, I have received sell-side job offers, and the interview experiences I had were quite similar. So though this book is written primarily for people looking for buy-side jobs, it should be useful for those who want to work on the sell-side as well (either permanently, or as a route to the buy-side).

Chapter 2

You Need to Have a Good Resume/CV and Cover Letter

In order to get an interview for almost any professional job, you need to have a good resume or CV. People tend to use resumes in the U.S. and CVs in the UK I am going to use the terms interchangeably as they are essentially the same thing.

When you are applying to a firm, your resume will usually be accompanied by a cover letter.

This chapter will focus on how to build a good resume/CV. It also touches on the cover letter. These two documents will get you in the door. But once that happens, the key will be the interview techniques described in the subsequent chapters.

A resume or CV is a document that concisely describes your educational qualifications, work experience, and other information that may be relevant to potential employers (like languages, awards, or publications). They sometimes also include a brief description of one's interests.

There are many books and websites out there that give advice on this topic (please see the Appendix for some books). I am going to give my thoughts here, but please feel free to consult these other resources for additional ideas.

Students should definitely seek advice from their university's career office or its equivalent. They often have useful resources and people trained to help you in this area.

After you have written your resume/CV, get at least one person to check it over carefully. He or she will pick up errors that you didn't and may have suggestions in the areas of grammar, phrasing, and overall content.

Don't ask too many people to look at it however; otherwise you will get confused by all of the different advice. In my opinion, you should get 2-4 people to look at your CV, maximum. Pick people that you trust, that can give you honest feedback, and that are in a position to help you. Classmates, more experienced students, former colleagues, and people who have already worked or are working in the industry you want to join, are good potential candidates.

Listen to the advice of your chosen advisors (and thank them for it), and apply it where it makes sense to do so. But in the end, you have to be comfortable with your resume, so make sure that the final product is yours and that you are happy to have it represent you to potential future employers.

Format of the CV/Resume

There is no one right way to write a resume/CV. The key attributes are that it must be clear, easy-to-read, concise, and consistent.

There are many existing templates out there which you can use - you don't have to reinvent the wheel.

Some business schools and universities will have a standard template that you can download or copy and then customize (check your career office's website). You might also find a template that you like on the web, or see friends' or classmates' resumes that you admire, and ask them if you can use the same base document.

Here are the most important attributes, in my view

- It should be 1-2 pages.

- In the U.S., where the resume is most common, it is always one page in length.

- In the UK, where it is usually referred to as a CV, you can go to 2 pages, maximum; one page is still fine, however.

- There should be no mistakes whatsoever in spelling, grammar, or punctuation.

- Make sure you use a consistent grammatical structure throughout the resume. For example, don't shift from starting sentences with verbs ("Managed university database") to starting them with pronouns ("I managed the university database").

- It should be well laid out, easy to read, and pleasant to look at.

Here are a few other points to note

- Use font sizes and textures (e.g. bold, italics) to emphasize categories, and create headings.
- Make sure to list your contact information on the resume, usually at the top, after your name.
- Start each sentence with a verb. This makes them punchy and conveys a sense of action. There are other ways to write a CV, of course, but I think this is the best way.

Please note that students tend to list their *Education* first on the resume, and then they move on to *Experience* (do check with your career office for advice on this, however).

People who are working tend to start with experience and then list their educational achievements later on.

Content of the CV/Resume

Now that we've talked about format for a bit, let's address the content of the resume/CV.

If you are an undergraduate, you probably don't have much work experience. That's understandable, and employers know this. Put what you do have, even if it's just working as a filing clerk in an office. It shows that you have done something. Of course, if you have had some interesting summer internships, list those. Mention it if you are a mentor, tutor or grader. You should emphasize extracurricular activities that you have participated in, especially if you had a leadership role. Some companies view this very favourably.

In the education section, list your high school (secondary school) qualifications, and your current degree program. Grades or GPAs should be listed unless they are very low.

Business school students should follow the outlines above, but may choose to leave out their high school and some of the more minor jobs. There is more emphasis on previous experience than extracurricular activities.

Experienced applicants may leave out high school/secondary school, but all university and post-graduate degrees should be listed. Listing your GPA is also optional if you are experienced.

Any relevant awards, accomplishments, publications, etc should be listed. You should also include language abilities and visa status/citizenship if they are relevant for your ability to work in a particular country or region.

It is also common practice to list some of your extracurricular interests and hobbies. However, this is the most optional part of your resume, and can be left out or given just one line, especially if you are short on space and trying to keep to one page.

In my view, having a "Personal Profile" or "Objective" section at the top of the CV is optional, though it can be useful in some cases.

Generally, as you progress in your career, you can start eliminating some of your earlier jobs, but only relatively minor jobs, summer internships, or jobs that you held for a very short time. All major permanent positions you had should be mentioned.

You should try not to leave gaps in your CV. A reader should be able to track what you have done from the time you left university until the present. If there are significant time gaps, you are likely to be asked about them.

If you are applying for equity research positions, you should emphasize any skills and experience you have that are relevant to the role, e.g. research, financial analysis, accounting, presenting. If you invest personally, mention that.

Remember, you can tailor your resume for different types of job interviews. You can have one resume that you send to investment management firms that mentions that you invest personally and have a $5,000 portfolio, for example. Then you can have another resume that you send out to management consulting firms (as an example), that doesn't contain this information.

Please note that you should be prepared to discuss anything that you have written on your resume in detail. Do not embellish or lie about your experience. For example, if you state that you are fluent in French, don't be surprised if a French speaker is sent in to have a conversation with you in the language, or maybe even to conduct the whole interview in it.

The best way to help you with your CV or resume is to show you examples. You will find some at the end of this chapter. I will give examples of both good and bad resumes. Hopefully, this will start you on the path to building one of your own. As I mentioned, there are many resources out there to help you, not the least of which is your university or business school's career office.

Format and Content of the Cover Letter

The cover letter accompanies your CV or resume.

It is always important, but can be especially so if you are approaching a company that has not expressed a desire to hire anyone. The cover letter is then a key part of your effort to convince the company to give you an interview.

The cover letter is addressed to the person to whom you are sending your resume, and should state the position you are applying for, why you want this particular job, and why you are qualified for it. It should mention that you have sent a resume or CV along with the letter, and tell the addressee how to contact you.

The cover letter should be written in a proper letter format. It should only be one page long. Other than that, there is a lot of flexibility in how it is written.

If you are in business school and applying to 15 companies over 1 week, you may want to have a rather short standardized cover letter than outlines the main points I mentioned above. However, if you are trying to break into asset management from a different industry, you may want to spend some time crafting a detailed, heart-felt essay about why you are making this career change and what you bring to the table. It all depends on where you are at the moment.

One warning for business school and other students however: if you are applying to several firms (which you should), make sure you don't make the surprisingly all-too-common mistake of forgetting to change the name and address of the firm you are applying to in each cover letter. If you just applied to Mr. Brown at ABC Investments, don't send a cover letter to Ms. Clarke at XYZ Capital Partners with Mr. Brown or ABC Investments mentioned anywhere within it. Do a search and replace in Word (for example) to make sure you have captured all instances of "Mr. Brown" and "ABC Investments" and replaced them with "Ms. Clarke" and "XYZ Capital Partners" as appropriate. You may not believe that anyone makes these mistakes, but they do. Some companies may still consider you if they receive an improperly addressed letter (maybe if you really do have an outstanding CV) but for others this will mean an automatic refusal.

You should tailor your cover letter for each industry you are applying to; it is more important to do this with the cover letter than it is with the resume. The same resume or CV can be used to apply to many industries, but you should have a separate cover letter emphasizing different points for each one, for example, one for buy and sell-side research, one for management consulting, and one for marketing.

I've given some examples of cover letters in the following pages, both good and bad. They are after the example resumes and CVs. I have not actually signed these cover letters, but you should sign yours, unless you are sending them electronically.

Please note that CVs, resumes, and cover letters should always be typed unless it is customary in your country to hand write the cover letter.

Example Resumes, CVs, and Cover Letters
Resume 1

ANDREW C. SMITH

20 Some Street, Apt 5 • City, State, Zip Code or Postcode, Country
(555) 555-5555 • asmith@internetprovider.com

EDUCATION:

2008-2010	**ABC BUSINESS SCHOOL**	New York, NY

Master in Business Administration degree, expected June 2010
- President of Investment Club. Publicity Officer of the ABC Graduate School Concert Choir.
- Member of European Students Union, International Students Union, Running Club.

2000-2004	**UNDERGRADUATE UNIVERSITY**	Chicago, IL

Bachelor of Science degree in Physics, June 2004. GPA: 3.5/4.0.
- Vice President of the International Students Union. Freshman Advisor and Tutor.
- Played on university tennis team. Member of Running Club, Concert Choir, Public Speaking Society.

EXPERIENCE:

Summer 2009	**COMPANY 3**	Boston, MA

Equity Research Analyst
- Covered five mid-cap European chemical companies for the International Value team.
- Researched industry trends, analyzed company financial statements, met with senior management at Boston-based Mid-Cap conference, built models, assessed valuation, made buy/sell recommendations.
- Presented industry overview and stock recommendations to several portfolio managers and analysts.
- Persuaded International Value team to take substantial positions in two buy-rated names.

2006-2008	**COMPANY 2**	London, UK

Management Consultant
- Worked on projects that spanned several industries including telecommunications, media, healthcare, and consumer products.
- Conducted research on industry trends, analyzed data, interviewed clients, competitors, suppliers and customers, developed conclusions, and presented recommendations to team members and clients.
- Operated in an intense team environment with other analysts and consultants, managers and senior partners.

2004-2006	**COMPANY 1**	New York, NY

Investment Banking Analyst
- Performed detailed financial and valuation analyses exploring the effects of mergers, acquisitions, corporate restructurings, and leveraged buyouts for companies in the healthcare industry.
- Examined company, industry and market trends.
- Created client presentations to illustrate analysis of strategic options.
- Prepared offering memoranda, working closely with company management teams.

OTHER:

- Founder of XYZ Fellowship for International Education and Entrepreneurship.
- Citizen of France and the U.S.A.
- Fluent in French, English, and Spanish; proficient in German.
- Avid tennis player, reader, and runner.

Comments on the Resume

This is an example of a good resume, in my opinion.

It is easy on the eye, uncluttered, with plenty of white space. However, it fills up the entire page.

The format is consistent from top to bottom.

Each sentence in the Experience section starts with a strong action verb like "Presented" or "Performed".

ANDREW C. SMITH
20 Some Street, Apt 5 • City, State, Zip Code or Postcode, Country
(555) 555-5555 • asmith@internetprovider.com

EDUCATION:

2008-2010   **ABC BUSINESS SCHOOL**   New York, NY
Master in Business Administration degree, expected June 2010
- President of Investment Club. Publicity Officer of the ABC Graduate School Concert Choir.
- Member of European Students Union, International Students Union, Running Club.

2000-2004   **UNDERGRADUATE UNIVERSITY**   Chicago, IL
Bachelor of Science degree in Physics, June 2004. GPA: 3.5/4.0.
- Vice President of the International Students Union. Freshman Advisor and Tutor.
- Played on university tennis team. Member of Running Club, Concert Choir, Public Speaking Society.

EXPERIENCE: Boston, MA

Summer 2009   **COMPANY 3**
Equity Research Analyst
- Covered five mid-cap European chemical companies for the International Value team.
- Researched industry trends, analyzed company financial statements, met with senior management at Boston-based Mid-Cap conference, built models, assessed valuation, made buy/sell recommendations.
- Presented industry overview and stock recommendations to several portfolio managers and analysts.
- Persuaded International Value team to take substantial positions in two buy-rated names.

London

2006-2008   **COMPANY 2**
Management Consultant
- Worked on projects that spanned several industries including telecommunications, media, healthcare, and ...mer products.
- ...industry trends, analyzed data, interviewed clients, competitors, suppliers and cu...
- ...recommendations to team members and clients.
- ...ts and consultants, managers and senior part...

New

25

Resume 2

ANDREW C. SMITH

20 Some Street, Apt 5 • City, State, Zip Code or Postcode, Country
(555) 555-5555 • asmith@internetprovider.com

EDUCATION:

2008-2010	**ABC BUSINESS SCHOOL**	New York, NY

Master in Business Administration degree, expected June 2010
- President of Investment Club. Publicity Officer of the ABC Graduate School Concert Choir.
- Member of European Students Union, International Students Union, Running Club.

2000-2004	**UNDERGRADUATE UNIVERSITY**	Chicago, IL

Bachelor of Science degree in Physics, June 2004. GPA: 3.5/4.0.
Vice President of the International Students Union. Freshman Advisor and Tutor.
Played on university tennis team. Member of Running Club, Concert Choir, Public Speaking Society.

EXPERIENCE:

COMPANY 3, Boston, MA summer 2009

Equity Research Analyst
Covered five mid-cap European chemical companies for the International Value team.
Researched industry trends, analyzed company financial statements, met with senior management at Boston-based Mid-Cap conference, built models, assessed valuation, made buy/sell recommendations.
Presented industry overview and stock recommendations to several portfolio managers and analysts.
The International Value team took substantial positions in two of my buy-rated names.

COMPANY 2, London, UK 2006-2008
Management Consultant

Worked on projects that spanned several industries including telecomunications, media, healthcare, and consumer products.
Conducted research on industry trends, analyzed data, interviewed clients, competitors, suppliers and customers, developed conclusions, and presented recommendations to team members and clients.
Operated in an intense team environment with other analysts and consultants, managers and senior partners.

COMPANY 1, New York, NY

2004-2006
Investment Banking Analyst

Performed detailed financial and valuation analyses exploring the effects of mergers, acquisitions, corporate restructurings, and leveraged buyouts for companies in the healthcare industry
Examined company, industry and market trends.
Created client presentations to illustrate analysis of strategic options;
Prepared offering memoranda, working closely with company management teams.

OTHER:

Founder of XYZ Fellowship for International Education and Entrepreneurship. Citizen of France and the U.S.A. Fluent in French, English and Spanish; proficient in German. Avid tennis player, reader, and runner.

Comments on the Resume

This is an example of a poor resume.

There is inconsistent formatting in the Education section: bullets, then no bullets.

There is inconsistent formatting in the Company 3 section: all the sentences start with a verb like "Covered" or "Presented" except the last line.

There is a spelling error in the Company 2 section: the word "telecommunications" is misspelt.

There is inconsistent formatting and punctuation in the Company 1 section.

There is too much space at the bottom of the resume.

Overall, this resume is not pleasing to the eye and not as easy to read as it could be. The formatting is not consistent from top to bottom, and there is a spelling error.

ANDREW C. SMITH

20 Some Street, Apt 5 • City, State, Zip Code or Postcode, Country
(555) 555-5555 • asmith@internetprovider.com

New York, NY

Chicago, IL

EDUCATION:

ABC BUSINESS SCHOOL
2008-2010   Master in Business Administration degree, expected June 2010

- President of Investment Club. Publicity Officer of the ABC Graduate School Concert Choir.
- Member of European Students Union, International Students Union, Running Club.

UNDERGRADUATE UNIVERSITY
2000-2004   Bachelor of Science degree in Physics, June 2004. GPA: 3.5/4.0.
Vice President of the International Students Union. Freshman Advisor and Tutor.
Played on university tennis team. Member of Running Club, Concert Choir, Public Speaking Society.

EXPERIENCE:

COMPANY 3, Boston, MA summer 2009
Equity Research Analyst
Covered five mid-cap European chemical companies for the International Value team.
Researched industry trends, analyzed company financial statements, met with senior management at Boston-based Mid-Cap confere
built models, assessed valuation, made buy/sell recommendations.
Presented industry overview and stock recommendations to several portfolio managers and analysts.
The International Value team took substantial positions in two of my buy-rated names.

2006-2008

media, healthcare, and consumer products.
... and customers, developed co

CV 3

JULIA A. SMITH

20 Some Street, Apt 5
City, State, Zip Code or Postcode,
Country
(555) 555-5555
jsmith@internetprovider.com

OBJECTIVE:

Sell-side equity research analyst looking to obtain a buy-side position in the United States or the United Kingdom.

EXPERIENCE:

2007-present   **COMPANY 4**
London, U.K.

Equity Research Analyst

- Maintain coverage of mid-cap consumer companies as part of highly ranked European Consumer team.
- Research industry trends, analyze company financial statements, build detailed quarterly and annual models, assess valuation, monitor news flow, make buy/sell recommendations.
- Maintain strong relationships with management and investor relations teams of companies under coverage.
- Write detailed industry and company reports, including quarterly earnings reports.
- Present industry analysis and stock calls to buy-side clients in the UK, Europe, United States, and Asia.

2006-2007   **COMPANY 3**
Boston, MA, U.S.A.

Co-Founder and CFO

- Founded this B2B consumer portal company that aimed to give very small and start-up consumer companies access to large retailers. Company was founded with former colleagues and classmates at Company 1 and ABC Business School. After finding insufficient interest from retailers, as well as severe competition from existing internet portals, the venture was wound down.

summer, 2005   **COMPANY 2**
London, U.K.

Management Consultant

- Worked on a strategic client project for a company in the consumer products industry. Conducted research on industry trends, analyzed data, interviewed clients, competitors, suppliers and customers, developed conclusions, and presented recommendations to team members and clients.
- Operated in an intense team environment with other analysts and consultants, managers and senior partners.

Comments on the CV

This is an example of a good CV.

It is easy on the eye, uncluttered, with plenty of white space.

The format is consistent from top to bottom.

CV 3

2002-2004   **COMPANY 1**
                      New York, NY, U.S.A.

                      Investment Banking Analyst

                      ● Performed detailed financial and valuation analyses exploring the effects of mergers, acquisitions, corporate restructurings, and leveraged buyouts for companies in the consumer industry.
                      ● Examined company, industry and market trends.
                      ● Created client presentations to illustrate analysis of strategic options.
                      ● Prepared offering memoranda, working closely with company management teams.

EDUCATION:

                      ABC BUSINESS SCHOOL
                      New York, NY, U.S.A.
                      ● Master in Business Administration degree awarded in 2006.

                      UNDERGRADUATE UNIVERISTY
                      Chicago, IL, U.S.A.
                      ● Bachelor of Science in Physics awarded in 2002.

AWARDS AND PUBLICATIONS:

                      Publication: *Need for Long-Term Investment Mandates in Modern Fund Management, The.* ABC Business School Press, 2006.

                      Runner up in Investment Club Stock-Picking competition at ABC Business School, 2006.

PERSONAL DETAILS:

                      Citizen of the U.S.A.

                      Permanent resident of the U.K.

                      Proficient in Japanese.

INTERESTS/HOBBIES:

                      Tennis, reading, running, music.

Comments on the CV (cont'd)

Each section in the Experience section starts with a strong action verb like "Present" or "Operated".

It is only 2 pages long.

Cover Letter 1

20 Some Street, Apt 5
New York, NY, 55555

25 March, 2010

Ms. Mary Baker
Human Resources Director
Asset Manager A
Street address
City, Postcode

Dear Ms. Baker,

I would like to apply for the Equity Research Analyst position that I saw posted on the ABC Business School Careers website.

I am a second-year MBA student with a strong interest in strategy, finance, and the markets. I believe that a career in equity research will enable me to fulfill my professional goals. I am particularly interested in a position at Asset Manager A because of its strong reputation and global reach. In addition, I believe that I possess many of the skills that you require for the role.

This past summer I worked as an equity research analyst at Company 3. I covered five European chemical companies for the International Value team. I carried out the full work of an analyst, including meeting management, making buy/sell recommendations, and persuading fund managers to invest in two of my buy rated ideas. This role confirmed my desire and ability to work as an equity analyst.

In addition, my past full-time work experience as a management consultant and an investment banking analyst have enabled me to develop the analytical, financial, and valuation skills that are key to the equity research role. I work well in teams, and have experience making presentations in a professional environment.

I have attached my resume to this application. It gives further details of my academic and work experience. Please feel free to contact me at the email address or phone number on my resume, asmith@internetprovider. com or (555) 555-5555, as well as at the address above.

Thank you for considering my application, and I look forward to hearing from you.

Sincerely,

Andrew Smith

Comments on the Cover Letter

This is an example of a good cover letter, in my opinion.

It is in correct letter format.

It clearly states the position that is being applied for.

The applicant has explained why he believes he is qualified for the role, highlighting relevant work experience and the fact that he is working towards an MBA.

Contact information is supplied.

20 Some Street, Apt 5
New York, NY, 55555

25 March, 2010

Ms. Mary Baker
Human Resources Director
Asset Manager A
Street address
City, Postcode

Dear Ms. Baker,

I would like to apply for the Equity Research Analyst position that I saw posted on the ABC Business School Careers website.

I am a second-year MBA student with a strong interest in strategy, finance, and the markets. I believe that a career in equity research will enable me to fulfill my professional goals. I am particularly interested in a position at Asset Manager A because of its strong reputation and global reach. In addition, I believe that I possess many of the skills that you require for the role.

This past summer I worked as an equity research analyst at Company 3. I covered five European chemical companies for the International Value team. I carried out the full work of an analyst, including meeting management, making buy/sell recommendations, and persuading fund managers to invest in two of my companies. This confirmed my desire and ability to work as an equity analyst.

... agement consultant and an investment ba...
... cation skills that are key ...
... in a profe...

31

Cover Letter 2

20 Some Street, Apt 5
New York, NY, 55555

25 March, 2010

Ms. Mary Baker
Human Resources Director
Asset Manager A
Street address
City, Postcode

Dear Sir/Madam,

I would like to apply for the Equity Research Analyst position that I saw posted on the ABC Business School Careers website.

As you can see from my attached resume, I am very qualified for this position.

I have a lonstanding interest in finance and investing. In fact, I did a summer job as an equity research analyst at one of your competitors. I also worked at an investment bank.

I am very interested in working for Asset Manager C, so please get in touch.

Regards,

Andrew Smith

Comments on the Cover Letter

This is an example of a poor cover letter.

The name of the addressee should be used, if known, rather than "Dear Sir/Madam".

There is a spelling error: "longstanding" is misspelt.

Fatal error: the letter is addressed to *Asset Manager A*, but *Asset Manager C*, is named in the body of the letter.

The ending of the letter is incorrect. Use "Sincerely" (in the U.S.) or "Yours sincerely" (in the UK) if you know the name of the addressee and "Yours faithfully" if you do not. "Regards" is not correct.

Overall, this cover letter is weak. It does not expand on why the applicant is interested in the job or qualified for it. It contains a spelling mistake and other errors of letter-writing etiquette.

20 Some Street, Apt 5
New York, NY, 55555

25 March, 2010

Ms. Mary Baker
Human Resources Director
Asset Manager A
Street address
City, Postcode

Dear Sir/Madam,

I would like to apply for the Equity Research Analyst position that I saw posted on the ABC Business School Careers website.

As you can see from my attached resume, I am very qualified for this position. In fact, I did a summer job as an equity research ...ance and investing. ...at an investment bank.

Chapter 3

How to Get an Interview

Now you have a fantastic resume/CV, and you have a draft cover letter that you plan to use when you apply to asset management companies (the buy-side) and maybe to the sell-side as well.

The next step is relatively simple: address your cover letter and send it along with your CV to each firm that you want to interview with. Hopefully you will get many positive responses back, inviting you to interview.

But how do you know where to apply? To whom should you send the resume and cover letter? This chapter will address these issues.

Main Ways to Find a Job

There are really only a few ways to find a job:

- Apply to companies that come to your university or business school to recruit students i.e. companies that come "on campus"
- Via networking
- Apply for positions that are advertised online (or in newspapers)
- Work with search firms or head hunters
- Apply directly (like cold-calling)

The methodologies that you choose to use will depend upon where you are in your career and the circumstances under which you are applying.

Notes for Students

The main target audience of this book is business school and undergraduate students. If investment management companies come to your campus, then the process is relatively simple. If they don't, you will have to work a bit harder.

Note that business school is a great time to try to make a transition to the buy-side. Asset management companies may be reluctant to hire someone who has experience in a completely different industry or function (e.g. marketing), or even a different branch of finance like investment banking. However, if you have worked in either of those industries and are now completing an MBA, those same firms are much more likely to give you a chance. Business school is an opportunity for a career rebirth. You still aren't guaranteed a job or even an interview, especially in a very competitive job market, but your chances have been increased.

Undergraduate students may find it difficult to get jobs at hedge funds right after they graduate. This is because many hedge funds are small and don't have the resources to train inexperienced hires the way some of the larger traditional asset management firms do. Hedge funds tend to like to hire people who have some financial experience, especially those who have gone through an investment banking program, because they will have received training in financial analysis and model building. It is also very possible to go from a long-only firm to a hedge fund. Some hedge funds will hire people straight out of business school.

Notes for Those Working on the Buy Side or Sell Side

If you are already on the buy-side, then getting another buy-side job will be a relatively simple process. It may take more or less time, however, depending on the state of the financial markets and the economy, and the current supply/demand dynamics of the job market.

If you are working on the sell-side, getting a buy-side interview should not be too complicated. There are some firms that will only consider people with buy-side experience, but many places are quite flexible. I have even seen buy-side job postings that explicitly request sell-side experience. Needless to say, your job is probably the most transferable to the buy-side of all other jobs.

Notes for Other Applicants

If you are not a student, but working in another industry and trying to get into the buy-side, the process will also be different for you, and I address this briefly. If you are not a student, and not working on the sell-side, you are probably in the most difficult position when it comes to breaking into the buy-side. It is not impossible, but it may take some time. Good luck.

The more experienced you are and the further your current industry experience is from finance, the harder it will be for you. This is because you are likely to be expensive (relative to a recent graduate) and people will view you as harder to (re) train and mould.

If you have been working in a different branch of finance like private equity, venture capital, or investment banking, it will be easier for you than for many others. Management consulting also tends to be viewed reasonably favourably by the buy-side. And if you have only been doing these jobs for a couple of years, then you are still viewed as reasonably early in your career, and it shouldn't be too hard to convince someone that you want to work in asset management, and that you can do well.

If, on the other hand, you have been working as a brand manager for a consumer products company for 10 years, it will be much harder to convince a buy-side firm that they should now hire you as an equity research analyst. You will have to make a very good case for yourself.

There are some firms, however, that specifically target experienced people with in-depth industry knowledge. An example is Sanford Bernstein, on the sell-side. Note that some other branches of finance tend to value industry knowledge as well. For example, venture capital (VC) and private equity.

General Advice: Cast a Wide Net

My first piece of advice is this: just try to get a foothold in the industry, don't just target the "top" firms. Almost any buy-side experience is valuable, so apply to many different places.

It may also make sense to cast your net wide geographically when you are trying to get interviews. This is especially the case for students, as you are probably more flexible in terms of where you can work, either full-time or for the summer. Don't limit yourself to the city or even country where you are from or where your business school is located. The key is to get a buy-side job. If your business school is in Boston, consider working in Denver, L.A., London, or Hong Kong. Sometimes family or personal preferences can get in the way – if so, fair enough. Work visa constraints can also be a pain sometimes. But many issues of this type can be overcome once you have a job offer. So go for it.

What's Coming Next

The rest of this chapter is divided into the different ways you can go about getting interviews. Depending on your circumstances, some sections will be more or less relevant to you.

On Campus

If companies come to recruit on your campus, then the process is as simple as it is ever going to be. Go to your career office or its equivalent, and submit an application to interview with the companies you are interested in. At some schools you may be able to do this all online. Typically, you will be asked to submit your resume/CV and a cover letter for each company. Make sure that both of these documents are of the highest quality - chapter 2 describes how to prepare them. If you are not required to submit a cover letter, however, don't.

If you have prepared well and have good grades and relevant experience, it is likely that you will be chosen to interview with some of the companies you have applied to.

In the event that you are not chosen by any companies (some years are more competitive than others), or if you don't want to just limit yourself to the companies that come to your university, you can apply to other firms directly. The next sections address that process.

Networking

What do I mean by networking? This is the process of finding a job through the network of people that you know. In the best case, you will hear about a job as soon as the position has been created and before it has even been posted or advertised anywhere.

Networking is by far the easiest way to get a job, but it is not usually a viable option for students who are just graduating, as they usually don't know anyone in the industry yet. However, if you are someone well-connected either through friends or family, you may want to try to use that network to find out about jobs that are available that may not have been widely advertised.

Some of you may feel slightly guilty about doing this, and it is of course up to you. But networking may be more common than you think – I've heard it said that as many as 70% of positions are filled by people who know other people. I don't know whether that statistic is really true, but even if it is half of that number, it is still a large percentage.

For those of you in business school, you may have a bit of a network that you built up during your work years. Previous employers, colleagues, and second-year students can all be good sources of job leads.

For undergrads, business school students, and almost anyone else, alumni can be a valuable resource. You can search your alumni database to see if any of them work at the firms you are interested in. It is a bit of a long-shot if you don't know an alumnus, but you could at least shoot off an email to ask if there are any opportunities at his firm at the moment. Most alumni will respond to current students (or other alumni).

Graduates and experienced applicants should also check their alumni job websites.

Use your university, graduate school, and business school alumni networks as appropriate.

If you are on the sell-side, you probably have the best possible network for knowing what's happening on the buy-side and what jobs are available. So I don't need to tell you to use it well.

If you are already a buy-side analyst, use the network of people that you know on the buy and sell side to find out what is out there. You may have former colleagues that have moved to other shops. You may have heard about an analyst at another company who has just left a position that you might want. The sell-side is actually very valuable at this time, particularly the salespeople. Remember, they talk to dozens of buy-side firms every week, so they are often the first to know if a vacancy has arisen. Ask them to keep an eye out for you.

This really does work. I once got a job offer after a salesperson alerted me to an opening. She told me about it because she knew I was looking, and the position was in the very same industry that I was covering at the time. I sent my resume over, interviewed, and got an offer.

Websites, Newspapers, and Online

Many companies use websites these days to post jobs. Often the jobs are actually posted by search firms on behalf of the company that is hiring.

These job websites will often feature positions that cater to a very wide experience spectrum, from university graduates all the way to very experienced hires, so they can be useful for everyone.

A popular financial recruiting website is efinancialcareers.com. Bloomberg also has a job listing section, which you can use if you have access to that application.

You can also check the job sections of financial and business newspapers like the Financial Times, Wall Street Journal and others that are local to you. However, like most things these days, job postings are migrating online.

Please do some research on websites that may specialize in your geographic area.

Head Hunters

Search firms, commonly referred to as head hunters, can be very helpful in a job search, but they usually work with experienced hires, not with people just graduating from university or business school.

That being said, for students, it would make sense to search the websites of some head hunters to see whether or not they do cater to graduates. If so, contact them. I have listed some of the major search firms that are involved in asset management in the Appendix (focus is on the U.S. and the UK).

If you do decide to approach head hunters, the aim is to try to get on their lists. They will often ask you to send them a copy of your resume or CV. Then they may ask to meet with you for an initial interview to discuss your experience and what you are looking to do next. The head hunter will then alert you if a position that matches your skills and requirements comes up.

Head hunters can often give you a sense of what the job market is like, as well as a realistic idea of the current demand for someone of your profile. That being said, many search firms are often retained by only a small number of asset management companies at a time, so it makes sense to talk to several search firms in order to get broader access to the market.

I have heard it said that it can be quite hard to get noticed by head hunters if your resume does not match exactly what they are looking for at the moment. One way to try to get around this is to be recommended by someone else. As an example, if you are working in private equity and you have had dealings with a particular head hunter before, it is likely that this person's firm will also have a division that deals with asset management. Ask your head hunting contact to put you in touch with someone in the asset management division. That way you are more likely to get noticed.

Cold-Calling

This is the least preferred option, but it is worth a try if all else fails.

By cold-calling I mean contacting a firm when you don't know anyone there, and the firm has not advertised a position, so you have no idea whether or not they are interested in hiring. It is a bit of a long-shot, but it could yield results, especially if you apply to many different companies.

This method may be more effective with smaller firms that don't have a formalized recruitment process. If a firm is already spending a lot of time interviewing candidates at universities and business schools that it has hand-picked, it may be less likely to pay attention to other applicants. But you never know, so you may want to write to the big firms anyway, just in case.

With a smaller firm that isn't actively recruiting, you may just catch someone who wasn't planning to hire, but who likes your resume and decides that they could make a space for you if they are really impressed. Again, you need to send out many applications and have a bit of luck for this method to work for you, but if you really want to break into the industry and nothing else has worked, you can give it a try.

Students might even consider offering to work pro bono (for free) for the summer to get their foot in the door. If you impress the company enough, they might offer you a job when you graduate. Even if they don't, you can now place "Equity Research Analyst" on your resume or CV, and this will help you to get interviews at other buy-side firms.

So if you do decide to cold-call, first make a list of companies that you want to target. I have created a list of some of the major buy-side firms in the U.S. and UK, but it is by no means exhaustive (see the Appendix). If you are in neither of those two countries you will have to start your own list from scratch. Here are some ideas: Google "asset management", "investment management" and "hedge funds"; look for investment management trade associations and note the members; ask classmates or second-year students who have worked in the industry for names.

I'm sure you can think of other ways to come up with the buy-side firms in your country – think of this as a research project. You do want to do research for a living, after all!

Note that many of the big U.S. and UK based firms will have offices in other cities, especially the big financial centres like Tokyo and Hong Kong.

After you have your list, visit the websites of the companies and/or call them.

You aim is to find someone you can send your resume and cover letter to. If there is someone in Human Resources (HR), that is often a good place to start. If not, you could try sending it to someone who looks like a decision-maker, e.g. the head of research or a portfolio manager.

Once you have a name and address you could just send your resume and cover letter and hope for a response. Better, to pave the way first, you can call and ask whether the firm will consider hiring you. If you get a flat out "no", you have probably saved yourself some time. If you get a "maybe" or "not sure", or "maybe in the future" you can offer to send your documents anyway.

When you call a firm, have a script prepared so that you are not at a loss for words. Keep it simple. Here's an example: "Hello, my name is Andrew Smith, and I'm an MBA student at ABC Business School. I'm interested in working for your company, and I'm wondering whether I can send you my CV". Of course, be prepared to answer why you want to work for the company and why you think you would be able to do the job.

In your cover letter you may want to mention that you are going to call in a few days to follow up. Once you're sure that the letter will have reached its target, do call. Have a script planned this time as well. If you get no response when you leave a message, or a clear, "We are not interested", then scratch the company off your list and move on.

Should you email your resume or send a hardcopy via snail-mail? It's up to you. I don't really have a definitive answer. Given the deluge of email that we all receive nowadays, some people will just automatically delete any message they get from an unknown source. Yet others may actually read all their emails and prefer being contacted that way. So you never know. I will say, however, that business people tend to get many fewer items via the post than they do via email most days. So sending a hardcopy might actually help you to get the attention of your target. Obviously, it is a slower process, but it might be worth it.

In the end, you have to weigh the pros and cons and decide which way to go. Of course, you could do both, to be on the safe side.

Chapter 4

Understand the Different Interview Types and Learn How to Prepare for Them

Now that you have prepared and sent out your resume/CV and cover letter to several firms, and been granted interviews with a few of them, you have come to the most critical part of your job search: the actual interview.

This chapter will guide you through the various types of interviews that you are likely to encounter at buy-side firms.

I start with some general interview tips, and then I delve into each type. This is the heart of the book and will be the longest chapter. Because of that, I have divided it into subchapters – I, II and so on.

I should probably make my most important point first, and hopefully it is an obvious one: you *must* prepare for your interviews. Finding a job is always a competitive process these days, and especially so when you are just graduating, because, let's face it, there are hundreds, even thousands of other people with quite similar experience and knowledge to yours, all trying to get the same jobs. This is particularly the case on the buy-side which is small in its hiring compared to many other industries. The only way you can really differentiate yourself is through the interview. You have to be majorly impressive.

So don't even dream about not preparing. Banish any thought that you can just roll out of bed, pull on a suit, show up at the interview location and wing it. Unless you are a young Warren Buffett in the making, that is a recipe for disaster. You must prepare, and prepare well for your interviews.

Please note that since the interview process tends to be similar on the sell-side, this chapter should also help you if you choose to interview for positions there as well.

General Interview Tips

My Most Important Tip

My first and most important tip is this: Prepare for your oral interviews *in writing*, and then practise out loud.

What exactly do I mean by this? Well, when you know that you are going to be asked several questions in an interview, sit down and think about what those questions are likely to be, and **write them down.** Don't trust your memory.

Once you have done that, **write down your answers** to those questions. Take your time and think carefully about what you want to say, as well as what your interviewer is likely to be looking for. I will refer to these questions and answers as your *Q&A*.

Finally, before you go into the interview, practice asking yourself all of your questions and then answer them using your pre-prepared responses **out loud.** Listen to how you sound. Are you speaking too quickly or too slowly? Are you beginning each sentence with an annoying "Ummm"? Are you stumbling all over your words?

Keep practising your Q&A until you have memorized them, and you can answer your questions in a smooth, confident manner.

If you prefer, you could ask a friend, classmate, or someone else you trust to ask you the questions, listen to your answers, and give you feedback. If you are new to interviewing, this is probably a good idea.

But how does this make sense, you may ask? Why should I write my answers down? What if I don't even get those questions? And won't I sound too rehearsed, like I'm making a speech, if I practise over and over?

I would say that even if you don't get exactly the same questions that you have written down, you are likely to get similar ones (provided you have done your preparation properly). Then when a similar question comes up, you won't have to go groping around in your head for the right answer. You will have already thought of it. That's the beauty of this method.

You can then answer quickly in a polished and professional manner. And of course you have to make sure you don't sound like you are giving a prepared speech. You might even want to pause for a bit to make it look like you are thinking of the answer on the spot. But in the heat of the moment and under the pressure of interviewing, it is unlikely that you will sound too rehearsed. That is likely to be the least of your worries.

Use the Career Office of Your Business School or University

Most business schools and universities will have some sort of resource that helps students find jobs for after they graduate. I am going to refer to this as a "Career Office" but it may go by another name at your institution.

You should definitely try to get help from your Career Office. This may seem obvious, but I was completely ignorant of the existence of this organization when I was an undergraduate, until someone pointed it out to me in my third year. Business school students are likely to be a bit savvier.

The Career Office often has lots of resources that can really help you during your job searching process. Specifically when it comes to interviewing, there may be people there who can do mock interviews with you, i.e. they pretend to interview you, ask you questions, and then give you feedback. This can be invaluable in helping you to improve your interview style.

All Students Should Join Clubs and MBA Candidates Should Talk to Second-Years

If your business school or university has investment clubs or hedge funds or stock-picking groups, you should join them. If there is a chance to participate, do so. These are good ways to practice the sorts of things you are going to do during your interviews in a (hopefully) non-threatening environment.

One of the best learning experiences I had in business school was joining the investment fund club. If I wanted to, I could stand up in front of the group and pitch a stock that I thought we should all buy. If I was successful in convincing a majority of the people, we would buy the stock with our own money that we had pooled together. Before I did this, I had no idea how to pitch a stock. However, I had learnt that this was one of the key things I'd be required to do during my buy-side interviews, so I made myself learn how to do it (I will go through how to do this later on in the chapter).

If you are in a two-year MBA course, you have an invaluable resource in the second-year students who have previously worked in asset management, or who are also trying to get into asset management, and have succeeded to some extent (e.g. they managed to get summer jobs).

Your classmates who've worked in the industry can help you as well, but since you may be competing with them for the same jobs, asking a second-year is better.

This is another reason why joining investment clubs is good – you are likely to meet like-minded second-years there.

Once you've met them, and identified the ones that are friendly and willing to help you, ask them for advice. They may be someone you can show your resume or CV to, and they may be willing to help you with interviewing, e.g. by listening to or reviewing your stock pitch. Don't impose too much, obviously, but do see if you can get someone to help you in the areas where you need it most.

Do Some Research on Each Company You Are Going to Meet

You should know something about every company you are going to interview with. This will help you to ask intelligent questions, and prevent you from saying something silly or inappropriate that could put your interviewer off and end your chances with their company.

I know that this can be hard, especially if it is interview week and you have three interviews a day for the next four days in a row (lucky you).

The more research you can do, the better. But in a case like the one above, make sure you at least know the basics. These include the investment style of the company (e.g. value or growth) if applicable, its size (in terms of assets under management), whether it is long only or long/short, its geographic area(s) of focus, and whether it is seeking to hire career analysts or potential portfolio managers.

You may not have to look far for this - a quick browse through the company's website or the background information that accompanied the job description will usually give you what you want.

Why is all of this important when you can ask your interviewers about these issues at the end of the interview, when they ask you if you have any questions?

Well, you need to tailor your answers depending on what the company does. When you are just graduating from business school or university, you are unlikely to have any real preferences when it comes to the things I mentioned above. You probably just want to get a good buy-side job. However, most firms are quite particular about these things, and it will matter to them if you have a strong preference one way or another.

So if you tell a firm that is looking for career analysts that you want to become a portfolio manager within 3 years, you are greatly reducing the chance that they will invite you to the next interview round or hire you. The same applies if you tell a long/short hedge fund that you think shorting stocks is immoral, or if you tell a boutique investment firm that specializes in small-cap non-US equities that your main desire is to cover large-cap US stocks at a big company.

The point is, do your research.

When in doubt, give a somewhat generic answer like "I just want a job where I can pick stocks. I am very flexible about things like geographic coverage and market cap".

Prepare Questions for the Interviewer

Most interviewers will ask you if you have any questions for them after they have finished asking theirs. Always have questions prepared. It makes it seem as though you are interested in the job and that you are curious about the company.

If you have done some research as I advised above, you will be able to ask more intelligent questions. But always ask at least one question.

Do not ask personal questions, anything that could embarrass your interviewer, or anything that could make you sound overly aggressive or critical. Unless the meeting has been specifically set up to discuss compensation, do not bring that topic up.

Don't ask something that the interviewer has already answered earlier in the interview. If you are really at a loss, ask a generic question that anyone can give an answer to. For example, "What do you most like and dislike about working in asset management/as an analyst/as a fund manager?"

Tips for the Day of the Interview

At the risk of sounding too motherly, there are some key, common-sense things you should do for the day of your interview:

- Sleep well the night before
- Eat appropriately (make sure you aren't starving, falling asleep, or overly
- wired on caffeine)
- Review your notes and other preparation documents
- Other – as you gain practice interviewing, you will develop habits that work well for you

Tips for during the Interview

There are some key things that you should and shouldn't do during the interview itself. Some of them are plain common sense. There are many books and articles written on this topic alone, and I have listed some in the Appendix if you want to research this in more depth.

However, here are a few of the most important ones, in my view:

Do

- Give a firm handshake to your interviewer
- Look him or her straight in the eye (unless it is culturally inappropriate to do so)
- Be polite and respectful
- Sit up straight
- Be professional, well-spoken, and articulate
- Wear a clean, well-pressed suit. No exceptions unless the company specifically tells you to wear something else. Suits should be conservative in style and colour. Makeup and jewelry should be understated.

Do Not

- Be late
- Swear
- Chew gum
- Be rude or disrespectful
- Wear perfume or cologne (can set off the interviewers' allergies or just annoy or overpower them)
- Babble. (Answer questions completely but succinctly. Do not allow yourself to go on and on. The more you talk, the more opportunity there is to say something silly.)

Chapter 4
Section (i)

Understand and Prepare for the Resume /CV Review Interview

Almost every initial interview you have will involve some element of this interview type, so you should always be well-prepared for it.

It is the "get-to-know-you" part of the interview, and usually comes at the beginning.

Typical Questions

Typical questions include:

- Tell me about yourself
- Why did you decide to go to this university?
- Why did you go to business school?
- Why did you choose to work in marketing after university?
- What did you like and dislike most about your previous job?
- Why did you move from working in private equity to a hedge fund?
- Please walk me through your resume.

Some other key questions that you need to be prepared for are:

- What type of job are you looking for? What is your ideal position?
- Why do you want to work in Equity Research/as an Equity Research Analyst?
- Why do you want to work on the buy-side rather than on the sell-side (or vice versa)?

- Why are you interested in equity research as opposed to management consulting or investment banking?
- Why do you want to work for us?
- Where do you see yourself in 5 to 10 years?

Some potentially difficult questions are:

- Do you invest personally?
- What do you think about the markets at the moment?
- Where else are you interviewing?

Experienced research hires should also be prepared to answer questions like:

- How do you go about analyzing a company?
- What do you look for when deciding to invest in a stock?
- What are the key drivers of the sector you cover?
- How do you gather information about the companies and industries you are following?
- Tell me about a recommendation you made that went really well and one that went badly wrong.

There are also other "standard" interview questions, however, these are not very common in buy-side interviews, I have found. Nevertheless, you may want to have a ready answer for them just in case:

- What is your greatest strength?
- What is your greatest weakness? (*please see the section below*)
- What is your most significant accomplishment?
- Tell me about a time when you failed.
- Describe a time when you took on a leadership role.
- Tell me about an ethical dilemma you faced and how you managed it.
- How would your last boss describe you?
- What would your friends say about you?

What Are Your Weaknesses?

I do want to mention that out of the list of standard questions above, the "what is your greatest weakness/what are your weaknesses" question seems to be the one that you are most likely to get during equity research interviews (maybe because it is one of the most difficult to answer). You have to come up with something that is a true negative, but not too negative. Don't try to be cute and give yourself a backhanded compliment like "I work too hard" or "I am so intelligent that all of my friends are jealous of me". Have a good think about this one and be prepared, just in case. An example might be something like "My organizational skills are not as good as they could be. I think that I could do a better job of filing my papers into relevant categories. That being said, I always seem to be able to find what I need quite quickly". This is just an example - you need to find something that is applicable to you. However, you should not mention a weakness in an area that is important to the equity research job or the company you are interviewing with. You should not, for example, say that your analytical skills are poor or that you are not comfortable with numbers.

What Are Your Interests and Hobbies? The Issue of "Fit"

It is also not uncommon for people to ask you what you like to do outside of work. This is part of the process of getting to know you, and should be relatively straightforward to answer. However, it is best not to mention any activities you do that could be controversial, or bias your interviewer against you in any way, e.g. political campaigning for a particular party.

Note that in addition to judging your technical and analytical skills, your interviewers are also trying to figure out whether you are the right "fit" for their company, i.e. whether your personality and habits will blend in well with the culture of the firm. This is quite a soft issue that you can't do much about other than prepare for your interviews well and be yourself. But you should be aware that you may be turned down for a job sometimes just because you didn't quite fit. This tends to be more important the smaller the size of the company. If there are only 10 people working together on a fund, they are likely to have a very strong culture and will want to make sure that the person they hire will get along well with everyone. If, on the other hand, you are coming into a large firm along with 15 other recent graduates, there will be less emphasis on personality and fit (though still some, mind you).

How to Prepare for the Interviews

I would strongly advise that you take some time to think about the answers you want to give to the key questions. You should write them down and then practise answering them out loud to yourself (or to someone else) until you can say them confidently and articulately.

When you are thinking of your answers, try to see the interview and the whole job search from the company's point of view. They are trying to gauge your interest, ability, enthusiasm, personality, and communication skills during the interview. They are also trying to understand the motivations behind the choices you have made in your career so far, and what that may say about your current decision to interview for an asset management position. You need to let your answers and the way you present them convey the right message.

Note that the company already thinks you have the appropriate level of experience for the job; you wouldn't have got the interview otherwise. Everyone else they are interviewing has the right experience too. So you have to shine during the interview.

Convince Them that You Really Want the Job

I think that one of the main hurdles you will face during buy-side interviews is convincing the company that you really want to do the job. For some reason, many people on the buy-side are a bit sceptical about the level of interest of potential new entrants to the industry. If you have been working as an analyst for five years, no one will ask you why you want to continue doing so. But if you are an MBA who hasn't worked in the industry before business school, you will need to do a bit of convincing that equity research is really what you want to do (as opposed to, say, investment banking or private equity).

So when you answer the questions, be confident, be positive, be serious, and be professional.

To help you with some more specificity in this area, I will give examples of what I think are good and bad answers to some of the questions I listed earlier. But first, let's deal with a few particularly tricky ones.

Tricky Questions

Do You Invest Personally?

Many interviewers may ask you this. If you do invest, that's great. You can talk about the investments you have made in your personal account (PA), and why you made them (if asked). So be prepared to do that during the interview.

If you don't invest, that's okay as well. I didn't when I got my first couple of jobs. Interviewers know that students often don't have the money to invest for themselves, even if they have the knowledge and desire to do so.

However, a good way to get some practice investing without using actual money is to build up a paper portfolio. This allows you to simulate buying, selling, and owning stocks.

There are free websites that allow you to do this, helping you to calculate your returns and track your performance. Examples include wallstreetsurvivor.com and bullbarings.co.uk; there are likely to be others out there. Then if you are asked if you invest personally you can say that you have a paper portfolio of stocks that you track. Be able to talk about what you own and why, and even how much money you have made or lost (on paper), just as you would with a real portfolio.

If you are taking part in a group investment club where you pool money with other people and choose stocks together, you can answer yes to this question about personal investing, but be sure to qualify it, e.g. "Yes, I invest personally through my students' investment club where we pool our money and make investment decisions together".

What Do You Think about the Markets?

This can be a tough question to answer because it is so open-ended. The good news is that there is no one right answer. The interviewer is likely to be looking for some demonstration that you are actually engaged and interested in what's happening in the financial world and in the stock market. The best way to keep up to date with this is to regularly read publications like the Wall Street Journal and the Financial Times, to watch financial news channels like Bloomberg TV and CNBC, or to just keep up to date with the market movements and financial news on websites like Google Finance, Yahoo Finance, and Bloomberg.com. Needless to say, there is tons of information on the web, for free.

Have a general idea of the current levels of major market indices like the S&P 500 and the Dow Jones Industrials in the U.S., the CAC 40, DAX, and FTSE 100 in Europe, and the Hang Seng, Shanghai Composite, Sensex, and Nikkei in Asia. You don't need to know exactly where they are to the nearest decimal point, but you should have a sense of what the trends have been over the last few weeks and months. If the market has recently had a major crash or if a large financial institution is on the brink of collapse, you should know about it. Is the oil price sky high? Has the British pound been crashing against the dollar? Is everyone talking about when the Federal Reserve is going to raise interest rates? You don't *have* to know these things, of course, but it could set you apart from other candidates if you do.

Then if someone asks you, "What do you think about the markets?" you can hopefully start talking fairly intelligently about one of the big topics of the day, and carry on a discussion for a few minutes. An example response might be "Well, the markets have been doing really well over the last 6 months, in almost every major geography. But I do think that it's going to be very important to see how the current debt crisis in Greece is resolved. It could have major implications for the market's confidence in the euro and for the European and global stock markets."

One final point: you may also find it interesting to read some of the classic tales of finance, books like *Barbarians at the Gate* or *The Predators' Ball*. They won't directly help you to get a job, but they will serve to acquaint you a bit with some aspects of the world of finance. I have listed some of these books in the Appendix.

Where Else Are You Interviewing?

Companies do like to ask this sometimes. Some of them want to see that you are really committed to equity research, and prefer to hear that you are only interviewing for asset management positions (and maybe also the sell-side).

I actually think that this is rather an unfair attitude for the companies to take. When you are a student, you have to find a job when you graduate, period. So though your preference may be to work on the buy-side, you have to do the sensible thing and interview for other positions as well, in case you don't get your first choice. This will probably involve interviewing on the sell-side, and some people might want to further hedge their bets by interviewing for other finance roles (VC, private equity, investment banking) or even non-finance jobs.

So what should you say if this question comes up?

I generally think it pays to be honest, i.e. mention that you are interviewing for other roles, but emphasize that your absolute first choice is to work as an equity analyst.

But I know some people think you should not admit that you are interviewing in other industries. They will stress that the firms won't be able to find out anyway. Maybe so, but I find that being dishonest often comes back to bite you in the end.

I'm of the view that if you are an exceptional candidate who really impresses a company during an interview (and hopefully this book will help you to do that!) they are unlikely to turn you down just because you are also interviewing with the investment banks (and you have clearly stated that you are doing this just as a back-up).

In the end, you have to make your own decision about this.

Examples of Good and Bad Responses to Common Resume Review Questions

Tell Me about Yourself

This question might also be phrased as, "Please walk me through your resume" or, "Why don't you tell me a bit about your background?"

Bad Example

Well, when I was fifteen years old, my parents decided to move from California to Colorado. The winters were very cold there, and I hated being outside. That drove me to love staying indoors during the winter months, and to reading. I began to read all day long, and eventually I started reading books about investing. Then I...

> *No one wants to hear your life story! Do not start with your childhood or teenaged years.*

Good Example

I did an engineering degree in university, however I realized in my junior year that I was also very interested in business and finance. I took a job at Tech Firm X after I graduated, as a software engineer. However I started to invest personally during my free time. I did very well with my investments, and decided that this was something I wanted to do as a career. I knew that doing an MBA would be a great next step for me to gain a lot more knowledge about business and finance, and also to transition my career to equity research. That's why I went to business school, and that's why I have applied to your company.

> *Succinct, relevant, shows a longstanding interest in stocks, and experience with (personal) investing. Note that the interviewer may ask you to delve into certain areas in more detail. Be prepared to do that.*

What Did You Like and Dislike Most about Your Previous Job?

Bad Example

Man, did I hate my boss. He was a complete workaholic, and I ended up pulling some really nightmarish hours. I think it's because he didn't have much of a life outside of work, and he felt that his underlings needed to suffer as much as he did. Plus the company was a complete mess, rife with infighting and political intrigue.

On the plus side, I really enjoyed wearing a nice suit every morning, and having a proper job on Wall Street.

> *Never emphasize the negative aspects of your last job, no matter how bad it really was - it makes YOU seem negative. And don't complain about hard work, it will give the impression that you are lazy. Don't give trivial reasons for why you like(d) your job.*

Good Example

Overall, my job was a great learning experience. There were parts of it that could become slightly monotonous at times, like creating pitch books. But I enjoyed the intense learning environment, and the great insight I gained into how capital raising actually works in the markets. I also did a lot of financial modelling work in Excel, and spent hours reading through the financial statements of several public companies in the media and telecom industries. I know that these skills will be useful when I work in equity research.

> *Positive, enthusiastic, emphasizes valuable skills; answers the "dislike" part of the question, but only very briefly, and then moves back into positive territory.*

Why Do You Want to Work in Equity Research/as an Equity Research Analyst?

Bad Example

I'm really interested in many branches of finance including sales and trading, venture capital, and corporate finance, as well as asset management. I just enjoy learning about companies and how they work, and I find the markets really fascinating. The good thing is all of these jobs give me access to that in one way or another, and I am interviewing for all of them. Plus they are all very lucrative career paths, and I'd like to make a lot of money in the future.

> *Even if you are looking at the possibility of working in many different areas of finance, this is not the time to mention it; in fact, the interviewer should have to drag that out of you. And when you are interviewing, as Michael Lewis so rightly said, "never mention money".[2]*

---

[2] In Liar's Poker, one of the best and funniest books about Wall Street, in my opinion.

Good Example

In my previous job as a management consultant, I found the strategy projects the most interesting, and I really enjoyed the research and analytical aspects of the role. In addition, I have a strong interest in finance and the stock markets. Equity research allows me to combine all of these interests. I will have to understand the markets and strategies of the companies I cover, as well as do in-depth research on their products, positioning, and financials. And finally, I have to boil it all down to a buy/sell decision on each company, and see how that plays out in the stock market.

> *There are many good ways to answer this question. If you can tie in your previous work experience, that's great.*

Why Do You Want to Work on the Buy-Side Rather than on the Sell-Side?

Bad Example

I think everyone on the sell-side is dishonest. The analysts have 90% buys on the stocks they cover, and that's ridiculous. Where are all the sell ratings? Plus they are all driven by the needs of the corporate finance arm of the bank anyway. The buy-side is where the true research is done.

> *Negative, arrogant, and dangerous. As I've mentioned before, there is a lot of cross-over between the buy and sell side, so you could be interviewing with a former sell-side analyst. Telling your interviewer that you think he/she is dishonest is not a good way to go!*

Good Example

Working on the sell-side involves other duties besides research, such as marketing and client service. They don't particularly appeal to me. I would rather focus on the stock-picking aspects of the role, and that's what I prefer about the buy-side.

> *This can be a tricky question because you are almost forced to say something negative about the sell-side, and you want to try to avoid being negative about anything during an interview. So don't belabour the point, just make it and be done with it.*

> *If you are interviewing with the sell-side as well as the buy-side, and you are asked where you prefer to work, note that you cannot tell your sell-side interviewer that you really want to work on the buy-side, and you are just interviewing with them as a back-up. It is never okay to say this to a potential employer.*

Why Do You Want to Work for Us?

Bad Example

I don't know, really. I saw you on the list of companies that wanted analysts for the summer, and I thought it would be a good idea to cast a wide net, and interview with as many places as possible. So here I am.

> *Even if this is true, it is not very inspiring for the company to hear. Why should they give a job to someone who is not really interested in working for them?*

Good Example

I'm very enthusiastic about working as an equity research analyst, and I know that your company has a great summer program that really trains and mentors people. In addition, your firm emphasizes long-term bottoms-up stock picking, and this is the type of investing that interests me.

> *You have mentioned something specific about the company. Note that the last phrase, "long-term bottoms-up stock picking", can be said of many companies, but it is still a valid point.*

Final Word

Some of the "bad examples" may seem a bit extreme and obviously inappropriate. I've done that on purpose sometimes, to make a point. But try to make sure that your responses don't contain even slight traits of the negative characteristics that I have included in my "bad example" answers.

Chapter 4
Section (ii)

Understand and Prepare for the Stock Pitch Interview

For business school students and experienced candidates, the stock pitch is an extremely common interview type when you are looking for equity research analyst roles. In fact, you could say that it is the core of most initial interviews. Therefore you should always have a stock or two prepared that you can pitch to your interviewer.

Undergraduate students may or may not be asked to pitch a stock. If asked, the level of knowledge required will be much less than that of a business school student. I address the undergraduates first. Others should move on to the "What is a Stock Pitch? For Business School Students and Experienced Candidates" section.

Undergraduate Students and the Stock Pitch

As I've mentioned before, asset management companies are typically open to hiring students that are studying many different subjects, not just business-related ones. Therefore, they realize that the people they are interviewing from this pool are unlikely to have the knowledge or experience to talk about the financial analysis or valuation of companies. However, they do want to test that these potential employees have the analytical ability for the equity research job. If you have a non-quantitative degree, especially, they will want to test that you are comfortable with numbers.

For these reasons, Case and Brainteaser Interviews (Chapter 4(III)) are quite common for undergraduate students.

However, you may be asked to pitch a stock by some firms, so it pays to be prepared just in case.

What is a Stock Pitch?

Well, the main job of an analyst is to research companies, figure out approximately how much they are worth, and decide whether or not their shares should be bought or sold. The analyst then has to present his or her views to others. The stock pitch is a test of how well you can do this.

What to Prepare

If you are interviewing for a long-only firm, you should prepare at least one buy idea that you can talk about. If you are interviewing for a long/short hedge fund, you should have at least one buy recommendation and one short (sell) recommendation.

Cues during the Interview

During the interview, you have to listen for cues to launch into your pitch. Your interviewer may say things like

- Tell me about a stock that you like.
- What company would you buy today, and why?
- What stock would you short today?
- Tell me about a company you like and why it would be a good investment.

Practise Your Pitch

Once you have prepared and written the stock pitch, which this chapter explains how to do, you should practice it out loud, over and over to a) yourself and possibly b) someone else. Practise until you can talk about the stock in a clear, confident manner.

How to Use the Rest of This Chapter

I outline a stock pitch in the rest of this chapter. You should read it, but note that some sections will not apply to you. In particular, you are unlikely to need to calculate financial ratios or come up with a valuation. There will be more of a focus on the qualitative reasons why you like (or dislike) a particular company, and your thoughts about the industry it operates in, its competitive positioning, and the quality of its products and services.

The exception might be if you are studying for a degree in business or finance. Then you might be expected to know a bit more about financial analysis and valuation. However, if you are interviewing along with all of your classmates, many of whom have non-business degrees, you may be given the same questions they are. Of course, your additional knowledge could help you to go that extra step and really shine.

So to prepare a stock pitch, undergraduate students should concentrate on the following sections of this chapter:

- Choosing a stock
- Make sure that the company is publicly traded
- Come up with a thesis, i.e. reasons why the company should be bought
- Think about what the risks to buying the company are
- Create a document that contains your entire stock pitch
- Practise out loud
- Prepare to defend your idea

After you go through these steps you will be prepared if someone does ask you if there is a company or stock that you particularly like. You will be able to talk knowledgeably about the company and give some reasons why you would invest in it. If you are challenged on your ideas, you will be able to respond. As I mentioned, you are unlikely to be asked about valuation (i.e. a calculation of how much the stock is worth).

If you do decide to do some valuation work, either by reading the other sections of this chapter or doing some work on your own with other resources, that's fine. But do not talk about things that you are not truly comfortable with during your interviews. If you start speaking about the valuation of a company, expect to be asked about it in more detail, and perhaps to be challenged about your assumptions.

If you are asked about a stock's valuation and you haven't done any work on it, you should just admit that.

Please note that if you invest personally, you might be asked why you own one of the stocks in your portfolio. Your answer to this question will be, essentially, a stock pitch. So if you do own a few stocks, be prepared to discuss them. Even if you own something just because you bought it on a whim or because it was mentioned on CNBC or because you inherited it from your grandparents, try to come up with some credible reasons for why you own it now.

To prepare your stock pitch, please now move on to the section called "Choosing a Stock", and read on from there.

What is a Stock Pitch? For Business School Students and Experienced Candidates

Well, your main job once you become an analyst will be to research companies, figure out approximately how much they are worth, and decide whether you want to buy or sell their shares. You then have to present your views to others. The stock pitch is a test of how well you can do this.

For the interview you must prepare a stock presentation that you will give verbally at the right moment, i.e. that you will "pitch" to your interviewer. You may then be asked additional questions about the stock and your views on it.

I will go into some detail about how you should go about doing this later on in this subchapter.

Cues during the Interview

During the interview, you have to listen for cues to launch into your pitch. Your interviewer may say things like

- Tell me about a stock that you like.
- What company would you buy today, and why?
- What stock would you short today?
- Tell me about a stock that you recently presented to your fund managers and that they purchased.

Practise Your Pitch

Once you have prepared and written the stock pitch, you should practise it out loud, over and over to a) yourself and possibly b) someone else. Practise until you can talk about the stock in a clear, confident manner.

How Many Stocks?

You are going to want to have 1-2 buy ideas. If you are interviewing with long/short hedge funds you should also have 1-2 short (sell) ideas.

Choosing a Stock

First you need to choose a stock. The truth is that it doesn't really matter much which one you choose. It just has to be something that you can present well and with conviction.

Choose What You Know and Like

A good strategy is to choose an industry that you like and understand. If you play video games all day long, then maybe you should try to pitch a gaming stock. If you love shopping for clothes, then maybe you should choose a fashion retailer.

Choose a Good Solid Company

There are a few guidelines you should follow, however. Make sure that the company is a good, solid one that is not in financial difficulty and doesn't have any major issues or controversies hanging over it. There may be times in your career when you do choose to buy companies that have some problems, but you may only have 5-10 minutes to present your stock, and the interview is not the time to be heroic. Of course, if you are preparing a short idea you may want companies that have problems of this sort.

You Have Many, Many Choices

There are hundreds and hundreds of companies to choose from, all around the world. Many of the products and services you use every day are created or provided by public companies. If you think about the technology you use, Yahoo, Google, Amazon, Apple, Nokia, Sony, Baidu, and Dell are all public. In household and consumer goods you have the likes of Proctor and Gamble, Colgate, Reckitt Benckiser, LVMH, and Estee Lauder. In food and beverages there are Coca-Cola, Pepsi, Danone, Nestle, and Anheuser-Busch InBev. In retailers you can choose from Marks & Spencer, Kingfisher, JC Penny, Walmart, Esprit, and H&M. In confectionery there are Lindt and Kraft. Public manufacturing companies include Caterpillar, Deere, Boeing, Siemens, Alstom, and Komatsu. These are just a few examples out of many.

Note on Financial Companies

Please note that companies in the financial sector (banks, asset managers, etc) have financial statements that are somewhat different from those of companies in other sectors. In this book, I will be addressing the analysis that is to be done on non-financial companies only. You should also be careful when picking a company to check whether it has a financing subsidiary attached. Some industrial and automotive companies, for instance, have finance subs which they use to help sell their products, by financing their customers. If you already know how to analyze this type of company, please go ahead. However, for the purposes of this book, I will be explaining how to work on companies that do not have financial operations.

Tailor Your Pitch: Value or Growth?

Another thing to think about when picking stocks that you are going to pitch in interviews, is that you want names that can be used for the many different types of firms that you are likely to encounter. As I mentioned in Chapter 1, asset managers have varying investment styles like Value and Growth. Ideally, you would like a stock that will be suitable for either of these styles. The key to doing that is to not go to either extreme, but to find a good, solid company that has some growth but is also trading at a reasonable valuation (a GARP strategy, essentially). Another approach would be to have 2 stocks prepared, one that is more of a value play, and one that is more oriented to growth investors. That might be too complicated, however, especially if you are new to all of this. Undergraduate students don't need to worry too much about this value/growth distinction, as they will not be focusing on valuation.

I'm Going to Use an Example: Colgate

Let's suppose you have decided that you want to pitch a particular stock as a buy. I am now going to walk you through an example, because that is the best way to illustrate how to prepare the pitch. For my example, I am going to use a company whose products should be familiar to almost anyone in the world: Colgate-Palmolive (ticker CL). If you guessed that the company manufactures Colgate toothpaste, then you are correct.

I am going to pitch Colgate as a buy idea. For shorts (sell ideas) you will need to adapt the example so that it makes sense. Please note that I have never covered Colgate during my work as an analyst, so the company is new to me. I thought I would move out of my comfort zone for this exercise, to get a bit of the experience of someone doing it for the first time.

Please note that all the data and stock prices I use will be as of March 2010.

Steps in Creating the Stock Pitch

These are the steps that you need to take to create your pitch: (Undergraduate students should follow the modified version outlined earlier in this chapter and only need to read the relevant sections that follow.)

- Make sure that the company you have chosen is publicly traded
- Do a quick check of the valuation
- Read the company's financial reports: annual and latest quarterly (at least)
- Calculate a few key financial ratios

- Come up with a thesis, i.e. reasons why the company should be bought

- Check the sell-side ratings on the stock

- Do a full valuation and calculate what the shares of the company are worth. This gives you a target price for the stock.

- Calculate the difference between your valuation and the current stock price. This will give you the upside (or downside) in the stock.

- Think about what the risks to buying the company are

- Think about catalysts: some events that could occur over the next few weeks or months that could cause the stock of your company to move

- Create a document that contains your entire stock pitch

After finishing your pitch there are two more steps:

- Practise out loud

- Prepare to defend your idea

Sell Side Reports Can be Useful

I'd like to mention sell-side reports here. Most stocks that trade on the major stock exchanges will be covered by the sell-side. Very large companies may have 15 or more analysts covering them, including those from the major investment banks like Morgan Stanley and Merrill Lynch. Smaller companies may have fewer analysts, mainly from smaller research firms. The key is that sell-side reports can be quite useful in getting some background information about a company and the industries it participates in. They can also be good examples of written stock pitches, especially if you are just starting out. So try to get a report if you can. You will want a long, in-depth company report or a coverage initiation, not just one that talks about the latest earnings release. That being said, the sell-side is just a reference point. Your recommendation should be one that you believe in, and it can be very different from that of the analyst or analysts whose reports you have read.

Where can you get sell-side reports? Well, if you are not already working in finance it can be a bit difficult. Sometimes your contacts in the industry can be helpful. Otherwise, you can actually purchase reports for some companies on Yahoo Finance, for example. (They tend to be from smaller firms, not the major sell side houses.) Depending on how much help you feel you need, you might want to consider that.

Colgate-Palmolive Stock Pitch

So let's go through the process with Colgate-Palmolive, which I am going to sometimes refer to by its ticker, CL. A ticker is a series of letters and/or numbers that uniquely identifies a company on a particular stock exchange.

Make Sure that the Company is Publicly Traded

Obviously, if you are sure your company is public then just skip this step.

You can use several websites to check. Google Finance is one that is good for US stocks (**finance.google.com**). If you go to the "Get quotes" box and start to type in the name of a company, matching tickers will come up. "CL" appears as I start to type in "Colgate". I click on it, and I see a stock price and graph come up. Next to the name Colgate-Palmolive it says "Public, NYSE:CL". This means that the company is public and it trades on the New York Stock Exchange (NYSE) under the ticker CL.

Mission accomplished.

If you have unluckily picked a company that is not publicly traded, you will have to choose another one. But don't despair, there are thousands of public companies, and you should be able to find one that is similar to your original choice. Let's suppose you love jeans and casual wear, and you decided on Levi Strauss. You type "Levi" into Google Finance and click on "Levi Strauss & Co". When it comes up you see no stock price. This means that the company does not trade on any exchange, i.e. it is privately owned. If you think for a bit, however, there are lots of other companies that sell clothes of this type, including The Gap, J. Crew, and Abercrombie & Fitch. You type "The Gap" into Google Finance and the symbol "GPS" comes up. You click on it and there is your stock quote. It is public. Google also lists similar public companies on the page, like Abercrombie, Urban Outfitters, and J. Crew. (Please note that this information is accurate as of the time of this book's writing; the website format may have changed since then.) You now have many other companies to choose from.

Do a Quick Check of the Valuation

Before you start doing detailed work on your company, you will want to check that the stock is not too expensive. Otherwise you could end up wasting a lot of time analyzing the company, only to realize that you won't be able to use it in your interviews after all.

However, I would not advise doing a full valuation at this point if you can help it, because you will need the input of the work you are going to do in the following steps of the stock pitch to inform your valuation work. You just need a quick screen to give you an indication of whether or not the company is cheap enough.

My advice would be to take a look at the p/e of the company on a site like Yahoo Finance. Then compare it to where the stock has traded in the past. This historical valuation range might be mentioned in sell-side analyst reports, or you can find it on a website like ycharts.com.

If the stock is trading within or below its historical range, then you are likely to be able to make the case that the company has valuation support. The further away it is from the top end of the range, the better. If the company is trading well above its historical p/e range, however, you may have a problem.

For CL, I take a look at the summary quote on Yahoo Finance. It gives information like the last trade price, 52 week range, volume, and market cap. It also has the "PE (ttm)" listed. I explain exactly what this means later on, but for now I note that with CL trading at $84 (in March 2010) the PE (ttm) is 19. Next I go to Ycharts.com, type in CL and click on the PE ratio chart. Scrolling down to the table on the left, I see that Colgate has traded on a p/e of anywhere from 18 to about 30. 19 is on the low end of that range, and so I feel reasonably confident that I will be able to make a good valuation case for the company.

This is just one way. If your studies or previous work have enabled you to come up with a quick way to estimate how much a stock is worth, feel free to use one of those methodologies and check that you get at least 20% upside from the current stock price.

Once you are satisfied that the company is cheap enough and will stand up well under a fuller valuation analysis, move on to the following sections.

If the valuation does not seem to stack up, however, you might want to drop this stock and start over with another one. Alternatively, you could skip ahead to the "Do a Full Valuation" section and do some more detailed work now to see if there is a case to be made for keeping your current choice of company.

Note that you will have to work hard to justify stocks that are trading on a p/e of 30 or higher. A rule of thumb cut-off for some value managers is 16. Some very high growth companies can get away with sustained multiples in the mid-20s and higher. But if you find a company that is trading on a p/e of 30, 40, or 50+, you might want to re-evaluate the decision to use it in your stock pitch. It is very hard to justify these types of valuations. You want to make the interview process easy for yourself, and starting with a very high multiple stock is placing an immediate hurdle in your path.

Read the Financial Reports

Public Companies Must Report

Publicly-traded companies are required to tell the world how they are doing on a periodic basis. In the U.S., they are required to file an annual report known as the 10-K every year, as well as 3 quarterly reports called 10-Qs. They file this with the SEC (Securities and Exchange Commission). Most U.S. companies will also have a separate annual report that they publish every year. Typically it has some of the information in the 10-K, along with nice glossy pictures about the company.

These reports contain vital information about the company: its main products and services, an explanation of the financial performance of the company over the year or quarter, and the financial statements, among other things.

The financial statements include a balance sheet, income statement, and cash flow statement. Hopefully you are already somewhat familiar with these from your classes in finance and accounting. We will talk about them more during the financial ratios and valuation sections of this chapter.

My advice is that you read part, if not all of the latest annual report for your company (if it is a U.S. company, I prefer to skip the annual report and go straight to the 10-K, but you may choose to read the annual instead). This will help you to get a good understanding of what your company does. You may even discover new things about a company that you thought you knew well.

I would also read at least the latest quarterly earnings release. In some countries, companies may only report semi-annually rather than quarterly, so read the semi-annual report instead. Note that U.S. companies usually release their quarterly and annual earnings before they file the associated 10-Q or 10-K. The quarterly report will give you a sense of how the company is performing in the near-term, and potentially some of the challenges it is facing, or opportunities it is exploiting.

Earnings Transcripts

You might also find transcripts of earnings calls helpful. Many public companies have a conference call after they release earnings. The management makes a presentation and then takes questions. The people asking the questions are usually sell-side analysts. Many companies webcast their earnings calls, so you can listen in live. They may also leave an archive of the call, as well as the associated documentation, on their website for a certain period of time.

You may be able to download a transcript of an earnings call that has recorded everything from start to finish. Reading a transcript is often more time efficient than listening in live. The Q&A section of the earnings call can help you to get a sense of what the key issues on the stock are at the moment, at least from the point of view of the analyst community. Two companies I found that supply free earnings transcripts for U.S. companies are seekingalpha.com and www.123jump.com.

To Do More Detailed Research

If you have a lot of time to prepare and want to be really thorough, you could read the last 3 annual reports, the last 3 quarterly reports, and also the annual and/or quarterly reports of the company's main competitors. This will enable you to understand how the company has evolved over time and whether or not it has kept its promises. Reading competitor reports will help you to get a better understanding of the industry, and how your chosen company is positioned within it.

Finding Financial Reports

Where can you find these reports? Most companies nowadays have a link to them on their websites. Try to find the link that says "Investor Relations", "Investor Information" or something similar. Then search until you find what you want: annual reports, SEC filings, earnings releases, etc.

For Colgate, I go to the website at **www.colgate.com**. I click on the link that says "For Investors". A menu appears under it as well as a page with information. If I scroll down, I see a link to "Annual Reports". Above that link I see a section called "SEC Filings", and the company has very helpfully provided links to "10-K Reports", and "10-Q Reports". It takes a bit more effort to find the latest earnings report. It is in the "News" section which appears in the "For Investors" menu. On the left, there is a link to "Earnings News". Clicking on that gives past earnings reports. (Please note that the layout of the website may have changed by the time you read this book.)

Reading the company's financial reports, along with your specific knowledge or opinion of the company, will help you with an important later step in creating your stock pitch, i.e. coming up with the reasons why you think the company should be bought (or sold) - the thesis. This will be covered a bit later.

If you have access to sell-side research, especially coverage initiations or other long reports about the company, it can be helpful to read them at this point.

Calculate a Few Key Financial Ratios

Use the Data in the Financial Reports

Each annual report will usually give you financial statements for at least two years – the current year and the previous one.

You should use them to calculate a few key financial metrics for your company. They are important indicators of the company's profitability and financial health, and your interviewer might ask you about some of them, and how they have trended over time. For example, after pitching your company, you might be asked, "What have the company's margins been like historically?"

Sometimes companies will include a section in the annual report that conveniently calculates many of these ratios for you, sometimes for as long as 5-10 years. Unless you are extremely sceptical or want the practice doing the calculations yourself, it is fine to use these numbers. If you want the ratios based on the latest quarterly data, however, you should calculate them yourself using the most recent report.

Example Ratios and How to Calculate Them

What ratios am I talking about? I have given a list of my favourites below, the ones I think are the most useful. They measure a company's historical growth, profitability, returns, leverage, cash flow generation and asset intensity.

This list is by no means exhaustive, so feel free to add or subtract from it as it suits you or as it makes sense for the company.

Hopefully none of these calculations are a complete mystery to you. If they are, then you will need an explanation of their significance, and you should consult a good financial textbook, as I cannot go into depth here. One book I would recommend is Higgins' "Analysis for Financial Management" (see the Appendix), which covers these ratios and others very well. However, you should find most of them in many financial text books.

Common financial ratios
- Sales growth: [(sales in period 1/sales in period 0)-1]
- Gross margin: gross profit/sales
- Operating margin: operating income/sales
- Net margin: net income/sales
- Earnings growth: [(eps in period 1/eps in period 0) – 1]; eps = earnings per share
- ROE: net income/shareholder's equity

- ROIC: EBIT (1-tax rate)/(debt + shareholder's equity)
- Debt/Capital: debt/(debt + shareholder's equity)
- Net Debt/Capital: net debt/(net debt + shareholder's equity)
- Interest coverage: EBIT/interest expense
- Free cash flow: cash flow from operations - capex
- Free cash flow/net income
- Capex/sales
- Depreciation/sales
- Capex/deprecation

Calculations for Colgate

For Colgate, I have calculated these ratios for the past 5 years and included them in a table below. You can do more years or fewer ones, as you wish, but it is probably a good idea to do at least 3 years, to get some sense of a trend.

Note that I got all of the data for these calculations from Colgate's 10-Ks, which are available for free on its website. I used its 2006, 2008 and 2009 10-Ks, with data from the income statements, balance sheets, and cash flow statements. There is a tremendous amount of information on public companies out there.

COLGATE PALMOLIVE, CL

	2005	2006	2007	2008	2009
Sales growth		7.4%	12.7%	11.2%	0.0%
Gross margin	54.4%	54.8%	56.2%	56.3%	58.8%
Operating margin	19.4%	17.7%	19.7%	20.2%	23.6%
Net income margin	11.9%	11.1%	12.6%	12.8%	14.9%
Eps growth		1.2%	30.1%	14.4%	19.4%
ROE	100%	96%	79%	100%	74%
ROIC	30%	29%	33%	36%	38%
Debt/Capital	72%	72%	61%	65%	49%
Net Debt/Capital	70%	69%	57%	61%	44%
Interest Coverage	16.3	13.6	17.3	32.3	46.9
Free Cash Flow ($ mill)	1,395	1,345	1,669	1,618	2,702
Free Cash Flow/Net Income	103%	99%	93%	79%	113%
Capex/sales	3.4%	3.9%	4.2%	4.5%	3.8%
Capex/D&A	118%	145%	175%	197%	164%

Conclusions of the Colgate Analysis

This data tells me that Colgate has been able to grow its revenues at a healthy rate every year except in 2009, which was a year of extreme global financial and economic crisis. Even then, the company's sales didn't fall, they just remained flat (0% growth). Also impressive is Colgate's margin performance. Operating margins have improved over the last five years from 19.4% in 2005 to 23.6% in 2009. The company was able to increase margins even during the financial crisis of 2009. This was obviously partly due to the jump in gross margins from 56.3% in 2008 to 58.8% in 2009 (a reading of the notes in the 2009 10-K reveals that the higher gross margin was due to higher pricing and a continued focus on cost savings).

Therefore, even though sales did not grow in 2009, earnings (eps) grew strongly, by 19.4%. Returns have been high and improving, with ROIC of 29% or higher. I found the level of debt rather high over the last 5 years, with a debt/capital as high as 72%. However, there has been no issue with CL paying the interest on its debt, as interest coverage has been very high, ranging from 13.6x to 46.9x. Given the stable nature of its operations, a company like CL is more likely to feel comfortable with a high level of debt than a company with more cyclical operations. However, the company has de-leveraged recently, with debt/cap falling to 49% in 2009 from 65% in 2008. This is not surprising given the general heightened concern over debt levels during the credit crisis of 2008-9. Finally, CL has consistently generated free cash flow over the last 5 years, a very good sign. Its free cash flow conversion (i.e. FCF/Net Income ratio) has been high, at 99% or more in 3 of the years, and only dipping below 80% in 1 year, 2008. The company has done this without starving itself of investment, as the capex/depreciation ratio has been over 100% every year.

Overall, an analysis of Colgate's financial statements shows that it is a highly profitable company that has grown earnings consistently, has a reasonably strong balance sheet, and generates a good level of cash flow.

Business Segments are Also Reported

Note that companies often report revenue and profit information for their business segments and/or geographic regions, as well as for the company overall. They will be reported in the annual report or 10-K, and often in the quarterly reports and earnings releases. If it makes sense for your stock pitch, you should delve into some of that detail as well.

Sell Side Views on Colgate

Because I have access to sell-side reports, I can get information from them as well. I find out that Colgate has close to a 45% global market share in toothpaste, and has very high shares in some of the large emerging economies of the world. The company is considered to be extremely well-run, good at product innovation, and disciplined about acquisitions.

The most pressing risk that the analysts are highlighting is the Venezuelan currency devaluation which took place in January 2010, and that will have an impact on CL's operations there. Note that the company has not been silent on this issue, and in its 2009 10-K, it estimated that the event would have a negative impact of $0.06-$0.10 on its 2010 earnings per share.

Another worry the analysts have is the underperformance of its Hill's Pet Food business.

If you don't have access to analyst reports, don't worry. You might have to work a little bit harder to get some information, but you can still come up with a credible stock pitch. There is an abundance of free information these days.

Come Up with a Thesis

You need to find 3-5 reasons why the company is attractive, other than valuation (which we will discuss later). Together, these points are called your thesis on the stock.

There are many, many good things you can say about a company, but do not just come up with a laundry list of generic items. Try to be specific, and if possible, try to say something that's not obvious, maybe even slightly controversial. Don't have too many reasons. Really boil it down to a few key things.

Thesis Examples

Here are some examples. For this exercise, I have stepped away from Colgate-Palmolive so that I can give a broad range of potential answers. I will use "Company X" instead.

- Company X has very strong brand loyalty. This makes it hard for new companies to enter the market, and enables Company X to keep its prices and margins high.

- Company X is doing extremely well in China. It moved in before anyone else, and is establishing a strong presence in this lucrative and fast-growing market. Its competitors will be hard-pressed to catch up.

- The new product that Company X launched recently is going to take the market by storm. I've used it and it is fantastic. I think it is going to have a very positive financial impact over the next 2 years.

- Company X recently exited its unprofitable lumber division. This will boost the company's margins significantly. It also shows that the management team is much more disciplined than the others in the industry.

- I am confident that Company X will be able to grow its earnings by at least 15% next year. However most analysts are forecasting growth of only 1-2%. When the higher than expected earnings growth is realized, the company's stock will react very favourably (*if you make a claim like this, however, you have to have the data to back it up, so be careful*).

Note that I have avoided very generic statements like "Company X is a good company".

As I mentioned, these are just examples. There are several other potential reasons to own a stock. Please think of ones that make sense for your company.

Of course, if you are preparing a short idea, you are thinking of reasons why the stock should be sold, not bought.

Industry Analysis Can Help with the Thesis

In order to help you come up with points for your thesis, you may want to start by thinking about the industry or industries that the company is operating in. Are they becoming more or less competitive? How fast are these industries growing? Overall, are these industries attractive ones to be in? Then think about how your chosen company is positioned with those industries. Is it gaining or losing share? Does it have a sustainable competitive advantage? How fast is it growing? The ratios you calculated in the last section (not applicable to undergrads) will help you to answer some of these questions. If you have strong views on the management team of the company, this can be a point in your thesis as well. However, unless you have been following a company for a while and know it very well, it is hard to argue this point.

Check the Sell-Side Ratings on the Stock

It is a good idea to see what the sell-side is saying about your stock. Yahoo Finance is one place where you can get this (check the UK site for European company information in English). There are other websites, including Marketwatch.com (for U.S. companies). Obviously, if you have access to a service like Bloomberg, you can find the analyst ratings there.

The Sell Side is Neutral on Colgate

For CL, I type in "CL" in the "Get Quotes" box in Yahoo Finance, and then when the quote comes up I scroll down to "Analyst Opinion".

I see that 15 analysts cover the stock and the average opinion is 2.5 (where 1 is Strong Buy and 5 is Sell; note that ratings are likely to be skewed towards the Buy end). The average target price is about $88.50. I can also see recent upgrades and downgrades by various sell-side houses. 6 of the 15 ratings are shown, and there is 1 buy or outperform; there is 1 Above Average (a rather unusual rating) and there are 4 Holds (also called neutrals, equal-weights, and market-performs).

Another website, Marketwatch.com, gives me the total breakdown of buy, overweight, hold, underweight, and sell ratings.

Overall the sell-side seems fairly neutral on the stock. That's fine.

Be Cautious if Your Stock Has Many Sell Ratings

It is good to check the sell side ratings just to see if there are any anomalies. Sell ratings are more unusual than not on the sell-side, so if you are about to prepare a buy on a company and you see that the ratings are almost all sells (a 4-5 in Yahoo Finance, for instance), you might want to pause and investigate why that is. Maybe the company is in financial trouble, or maybe it is extremely overvalued.

In general, whether or not the company has many sell ratings; sell-side reports can be quite useful for picking some of these problems up. A long, detailed, recent report on the company is likely to highlight issues like high levels of debt, excessive management turnover, court cases, asbestos liabilities, etc.

Another reason why a stock might have many sell ratings is that the ratings could be stale, i.e. the company was in trouble, but is staging a turnaround, and you have picked it up before the analysts have changed their opinions. It's possible, but turnaround stories can be hard to prove or convince someone else about. You might want to pitch an easier stock in that case. If you are really convinced about your argument, however, you should stick to it.

In fact, some people will argue that when everyone hates a company, that's the time to be contrarian and buy it. I say maybe and maybe not.

Remember, your aim at this point is not to find the best stock idea in the world, one that is going to triple in value in 6 months, for example. Save that for when you actually are an analyst. Right now you want to find a stock that you can easily and confidently pitch during an interview, one that will impress your interviewer enough to invite you back for the next round. Coming up with a widely out-of-favour controversial idea may not serve that purpose.

The more experienced you are, the more you can disregard this advice and really go for the killer idea. But if you are a student with not much stock-picking experience, you will want to stick with something "safer".

Do a Full Valuation - Calculate What the Shares of the Company Are Worth

This is a very important part of your stock pitch, and it is the most technical part of it. It involves looking at the company's financial statements, potentially building a financial model for the company, and calculating how much it is worth.

There are whole books and university courses on just this subject alone. I am going to focus on one main methodology here, using p/e multiples. If you want to study the topic in more depth, please see the resources listed in the Appendix. If you are a student, you can use the textbooks from the relevant courses at your university (or borrow them from someone who is taking the courses).

Sell-side reports can also be very useful with valuation. Most reports will include a section on this key topic, and you can use this as a guide for the most common metrics that are used to evaluate your company.

Don't Pitch an Expensive Stock

Assuming that you are preparing a buy rating, you need to show that your company is attractively valued. If after you do your valuation work you find that your company is clearly expensive or over-valued, then I suggest that you ditch the idea and start with a new one. If you are preparing a short, however, the opposite applies, of course.

Each Asset Manager Will Have a Preferred Valuation Methodology

There are many ways to value a company, but two common ways are

- Multiples like p/e, p/b, EV/EBITDA, EV/Sales
- A discounted cash flow (DCF) analysis

If you know how to do a DCF from your previous experience or from class work, and you have the time, you could build one for your company. However, I would still do a multiples valuation as well.

Please note: some asset managers have very strong feelings about which valuation methods are appropriate for valuing public companies. For example, some value managers dislike DCF and will focus on metrics like p/e and p/b. However, other firms rely very heavily on DCF and use it as their primary valuation methodology. Yet other companies may prefer multiples, and only use DCF as a back-up. If you can, try to find out if the company you are interviewing with has any strong views, so that you do not present them with a valuation methodology that they will instantly reject. You can sometimes find the methods the companies prefer on their websites.

Generally, using p/e is a safe method; most firms seem to accept it.

The P/E Ratio

To calculate this ratio, the basic method is that you look at the earnings per share (eps) of a company, the "e" in the equation, and compare it with the current stock price, the "p". The ratio of the two is the p/e. So if your stock has a price of $28, and it earned $2.00 per share, the p/e is 14.

For the eps, you can use the most recently reported number, but more typically, analysts like to look at the earnings the company is expected to make in the next year or in the year after that. When the current price is divided by future estimated earnings, it is called a "forward p/e". If the last reported 4 quarters of earnings are used, it is called a "trailing p/e".

Where to Find Earnings Data

Where can you find what your company is estimated to earn next year? Well, you can either build a model for the company yourself and estimate it, or you can rely on the sell-side "consensus" number.

If you know how to build a model (well) and have the time, then great, go ahead and do so. You can then speak with more authority during the interview and say "I estimate that Company X will earn $2.00 per share next year".

However, I think it is okay to use the consensus number during a stock pitch interview (unless your entire thesis is built on the fact that the sell-side is under-estimating or over-estimating the company's earnings).

Where does the consensus number come from? Well the analysts that cover the stock will publish their estimates of what the company is going to earn over the next few quarters and years. This is aggregated and averaged, and gives you the consensus number. You can find this number on paid services like Bloomberg, or for free on sites like Yahoo Finance (check the US site for US companies and the UK site for European companies) or Marketwatch.com.

Calculating Colgate's P/E

For CL, I look on Yahoo Finance and see that the average earnings estimate for the current year (ended December 2010) is $4.85 and for the year ended December 2011 it is $5.36. The current stock price of CL is about $84, so it is trading on a p/e of 17.3x 2010 earnings and 15.7x 2011 earnings. Note that the 19x number that was mentioned in the earlier "Do a Quick Valuation Check" section was a trailing p/e (TTM stands for trailing twelve months). Colgate's earnings in 2009 were $4.37. $84/$4.37 = 19.2, so now you can see where that number came from.

Please note that the numbers quoted here are as of March 2010, and of course they may have changed by the time you read this book.

It is a good idea for you to keep a spreadsheet for your stock that has some of this key information. Stock prices can change quickly. As long as CL is trading in the $83-85 range, I am happy to say it is trading at around $84, and use these p/e numbers in my stock pitch. But if the stock fell to $80 or rose to $88, for example, I would want to modify my p/e.

Is Colgate Expensive or Cheap?

So CL is trading on a forward p/e of about 16x (using 2011). Is that expensive or cheap? Well, this is the key question of the day. There are many ways to try to answer this, each with its pros and cons:

- I could look at where CL is trading relative to some of its competitors like Proctor & Gamble (PG) and Clorox (CLX). If it is trading at a lower multiple, I could argue that it deserves to be at least in line with them. The pro is that this is relatively easy to do. The problem is that there may be legitimate reasons why other companies are trading at higher multiples – they may have better growth rates, or higher profitability, or better management.

- I could look at where CL is trading relative to its own history. For example, if it has historically (over the last 5-10 years) traded on a p/e of 17-18x, and is now only at 16x (the "x" stands for "times"); I can argue that it is cheap. This can be quite a good argument. The pitfall is if the company has significantly changed in a way that has caused it to now get a lower multiple. I also need to have some opinion as to why the company is now trading cheaply. But that's not necessarily a problem. I could say, for instance, that, "the market is concerned at the moment about the company's manufacturing problems in Vietnam, which is why the stock is trading at a discount. However, I think that these problems will soon be fixed, and the company will regain its historical multiple". I am just making this up as an example, but I hope you get my point.

- I could see where CL is trading relative to the market. If it is trading at a discount to what it has historically, I can argue that it should get back to the average. This involves looking at a "relative p/e". That is, you are not looking at the absolute p/e of the stock, but how that p/e compares with the p/e of the market. For CL, an appropriate measure of the market would be a broad US index like the S&P 500. If you are analyzing a non-US stock, you will want to use the appropriate index, e.g. the Topix in Japan.

- I could see where CL is trading relative to its growth rate. This involves calculating what is called the PEG ratio, i.e. the Price/Earnings to Growth ratio. I look at what the p/e is, and what the growth rate in CL's earnings is expected to be, typically over the next year or next 5 years. It is a rule of thumb that a PEG ratio below 1 is cheap, and a PEG ratio above 1 is expensive. I haven't used this method much and don't particularly like it, but it is potentially another weapon in your valuation arsenal.

- If none of this works, and CL is trading above its historical ranges on all of these metrics, I could argue that the company is improving and becoming much better than it was in the past (in terms of growth, profitability, etc), and so it deserves a higher valuation than it has ever had in the past. But this is a tough one to argue, so I would avoid it, if possible.

Note that if your stock is trading **at** its historical multiples, rather than below them, you can still argue that it is trading at a reasonable or attractive valuation, especially if it is a company that is performing well and growing quickly. If a stock is trading at its average multiple, but it is going to grow earnings 25% per year, then if you multiply the next year's earnings by the same average multiple, you will automatically get 25% upside. You are making the assumption here that the stock can maintain this multiple for at least the next year.

The more ways the stock looks cheap, the better. So if you can argue that your stock looks cheap relative to its history and its competitors, then it's better than if it just looks cheap relative to its competitors.

Valuation is Both Art and Science

At the end of the day, valuation is a bit of an art as well as a science. You can probably find a way to argue that almost any stock looks cheap on some metric. But do yourself a favour and find a company where the argument is easy and readily apparent. Remember, your interviewer is likely to be much more experienced than you are, and the last thing you want is to have him or her jumping all over you and challenging your valuation analysis during the interview.

That happened to me once, by the way. I presented a stock and said that it was trading at a discount to the market, and historically it had traded at or above the market, so it looked cheap. My interviewer immediately said that he did not at all agree with the methodology of valuing a stock based on how it traded relative to the market, that he thought it was a really flawed analysis. I was early in my career and couldn't really argue with him, so I didn't. Sometimes, no matter how well you prepare, you will run into someone who just disagrees with you. But don't let that stop you from preparing!

Be Careful Valuing Cyclical Companies

Be careful with cyclical companies and ratios like p/e. If a company is very cyclical and its earnings tend to, for example, fall 50% from peak to trough and then rebound again every few years, then you need to make sure to take that into account when you are doing the valuation. You commonly find companies like this in the industrial and materials sectors. The market tends to give these companies a low p/e multiple when the earnings are high (i.e. at or close to peak earnings) and a high p/e multiple when the earnings are low, or at a trough. This is because the market recognizes that the peak earnings are unsustainable, and consequently won't pay too much for them. Correspondingly, the market realizes that when the earnings are at a trough, they are likely to eventually rise, and the multiple expands to compensate for that. So try to make sure that you don't do the opposite, e.g. assign a very high multiple to a cyclical company that is trading at or near peak earnings. Analyst reports will often tell you what the historical range has been at both peaks and troughs, and you can use that range. If the company is not trading at a peak or a trough, but somewhere in between, it is said to be mid-cycle, and then you want to give it a mid-cycle or average multiple. If all of this is too confusing, try not to pick a very cyclical company. Colgate, for example, is not very cyclical at all. In fact it is the opposite; it is considered a consumer staple. Staple companies tend to have less volatility in their earnings than cyclical companies.

Other companies you could pick would be classic growth stocks, i.e. companies that tend to consistently growth their earnings year in year out, maybe with the occasional hiccup in performance, but with an overall strong trend. Note that CL, though a consumer staple, exhibits these characteristics.

Is Colgate a Value or Growth Stock?

It is also worth considering whether CL would be classified as a value or a growth stock from a valuation point of view. I described these investing styles in Chapter 1. The stock is trading on a forward p/e of 16x and a trailing p/e of 19x. A rule of thumb cut-off for value managers is a 16x trailing p/e, so CL is trading a bit high to be classified as a value name. However it is not wildly expensive either. It also has the type of consistency of performance and strong cash flow generation that is often sought by value investors. On the growth side of things, the company has had double-digit earnings growth for 3 straight years, though the last 2 years have been in the teens, not 20%+ or 30%+. Overall, CL would probably sit comfortably in the GARP basket (growth at a reasonable price). This has the advantage that it would probably be acceptable to both value and growth asset managers if presented as a stock pitch during an interview.

Finding Historical P/E Data

So, where can you find data on competitor, historical, and market p/e multiples?

If you have access to a service like Bloomberg, then you can find these metrics there. Most students will want to use free sites, however, and I list below a few that I know of. Please look for others according to your needs.

Also, please note that finding company p/e data is relatively easy; it is finding (free) market and market relative p/e multiples that is a bit harder. You may have to find the market p/e and then divide your company's p/e by the market's to find the relative p/e ratio, and you'll have to do this many times to get a time series. But if you are going to be an equity analyst, you can't be afraid of a bit of mathematics, and you may as well start now.

Where to find historical and market p/e data

- Yahoo Finance: For U S companies, in the "Analyst Estimates" section it gives the Price/Earnings of the company, industry, sector and market (the S&P 500 in the case of CL)

- Ycharts.com: charts and tables of various ratios, including p/e. This site also focuses on U S stocks

- **www.multpl.com**: gives the p/e ratio of the S&P 500 in chart and table form over several years

Colgate's PEG Ratio

Note that Yahoo Finance even calculates the PEG ratio for you. At the bottom of the "Analyst Estimates" section, it gives the p/e, expected growth over the next 5 years, and the resulting p/e to growth or PEG ratio. At the time of writing, this was 1.82 for CL, above 1 and above the 1.24 PEG ratio of the industry (also calculated by Yahoo). So obviously I would not use this metric in my buy case for CL.

Using Financial Statements in the Valuation

While you are doing your valuation, you may find it useful to refer to the quarterly and annual financial statements to get information like historical earnings. If you are doing a DCF, you will need the financial statements to start off the building of your model.

P/E Valuation for Colgate

Let's finish off my valuation for CL. At $84, the stock is trading on a p/e multiple of about 16x consensus 2011 earnings of $5.36. Over the last 10 years, however, the stock has traded on a multiple range of 18-30x. I can see this from a website like Ycharts.com. If the stock were to trade on the low end of that range, on 19x 2011 earnings, it would be worth $102 per share (19*$5.36 = $101.84).

So, I am going to use $102 as my valuation.

Why am I using a p/e of 19 as opposed to 18 or 30 or any other number in between, you may ask.

The truth is that there isn't one definitive answer to that question. Theoretically, I could have used any number in that range. I chose 19 because it is on the low end of the range and therefore I could argue that I am being conservative in my valuation. The opposite of being "conservative" in the investment world is being "aggressive". It would have been considered aggressive if I had picked a number on the high end of the 18-30 range as my p/e, for example 28 or 30. This is because I can't guarantee that 30 is a multiple that Colgate deserved or that it will return to or that can be sustained in the future. Therefore using a 30 multiple would be assuming a best case scenario, and therefore aggressive.

Instead of 19, I could have used the midpoint of the 18-30 range i.e. a p/e of 24. This would be a balanced strategy and also plausible.

However, as I mentioned, valuation is part art, part science. If I had a good, convincing argument as to why CL should now trade on the high end of its historical range, I could use it. Therefore theoretically, using this methodology, I could say that the stock was worth anything from $97 per share (18*$5.36 = $96.48) to $161 per share (30* $5.36 = $160.80).

Bear in mind that there is rarely one "true" valuation for any company - there are just too many unknown variables. Who can really say with 100% certainty what a company is going to earn in 1 year's time, and what p/e multiple it should trade on? At best, we can try to come somewhere in the range of what a company is worth. And so there is some leeway when you are doing your valuation.

In this case, I have decided to be conservative and pick a number that is close to but not exactly at the low end of the range i.e. a p/e of 19.

Comparables Valuation for Colgate

I also want to get a sense of where CL is trading relative to its peers. This is called doing a "comps" analysis (for comparables). I use current stock prices and consensus estimates for 2010 and 2011 for these companies as well as CL to get their p/e multiples. Once again, I have obtained this data from Yahoo Finance.

The comps I am using are other large consumer staple companies: Procter & Gamble (PG), Coca Cola (KO), Pepsi (PEP), General Mills (GIS), Clorox (CLX) and Kimberly Clark (KMB).

	Price	Consensus eps 2010	Consensus eps 2011	P/E 2010	P/E 2011
PG	63	4.14	4.06	15.2	15.5
KO	53	3.42	3.73	15.5	14.2
PEP	65	4.17	4.64	15.6	14.0
GIS	72	4.60	4.99	15.7	14.4
CLX	63	4.24	4.64	14.9	13.6
KMB	60	4.91	5.32	12.2	11.3
Average	n/a	n/a	n/a	14.8	13.8
CL	84	4.85	5.36	17.3	15.7

This analysis shows me that CL is trading at a bit of a premium to its peers. However, CL has higher profitability and better near-term growth prospects than its comparable companies, so it can be argued that this premium is justified. To see what the growth prospects are for each company, calculate the growth rate from the earnings estimates for 2010 and 2011 (see table below). To compare the profitability of the companies, look at measures like operating margin, ROE, and ROA. You can get this by going through the financial statements of each company. As a short-hand, Yahoo Finance calculates some of these metrics on its "Key Statistics" page for each stock.

	Price	Consensus eps 2010	Consensus eps 2011	P/E 2010	P/E 2011	eps growth rate
PG	63	4.14	4.06	15.2	15.5	-2%
KO	53	3.42	3.73	15.5	14.2	9%
PEP	65	4.17	4.64	15.6	14.0	11%
GIS	72	4.60	4.99	15.7	14.4	9%
CLX	63	4.24	4.64	14.9	13.6	9%
KMB	60	4.91	5.32	12.2	11.3	8%
Average	n/a	n/a	n/a	14.8	13.8	7%
CL	84	4.85	5.36	17.3	15.7	11%

Calculate the Difference Between Your Valuation and the Current Stock Price. This Will Give You the Upside (or Downside) in the Stock

This step is really simple but has big implications. I need to take my valuation from the previous section, check it with where the stock is currently trading, and calculate the percentage difference. Note that the derived valuation is often called a "target price".

For Colgate:

My valuation: $102

Current stock price: $84

Upside: 21% (102/84 – 1)

Have At Least 15-20% Upside

If you are making a buy case for a stock, you should probably have at least 20% upside. If it is a very high quality, solid, company, with not much risk, you can probably get away with 15% upside. If you are pitching a high growth, rather risky company, you should aim for more upside, like 30%+.

These are just guidelines, you can move somewhat within them. But definitely do not come to the table with a stock that has less than 10% upside. It is really not worth it at that point.

If you are shorting a stock, of course you are looking for downside, not upside. I would also make sure that your downside is significant.

If you have done your valuation and even under the most aggressive scenarios you don't have enough upside, then you should give up on the idea and start over with another one. However hopefully this will not happen to you given the quick valuation check that you did at the beginning of the stock pitch.

Think About What the Risks to Buying the Company Are

Buying any stock involves risks, and you need to know what the key ones are for your chosen company.

Do not come up with a laundry list of every possible thing that could happen under the sun. You need the 2-5 things that could really go wrong and affect the company and its share price. Some of these may be risks that are inherent to any company in that industry.

If you are buying a stock or going long, you want to think of things that may make the stock go down. And if you are shorting, you are obviously looking for the opposite.

Check Annual and Sell Side Reports for Risks

Note that most companies will list what they consider to be risks to their operations in their annual reports. You can take a look at these lists, but note that, on the one hand, they tend to be a sort of legal disclaimer catch-all of everything that could go wrong. On the other hand, they may not contain some of the most recent and important developments that the market is worried about where that company is concerned.

Sell-side reports can be useful here because they almost always list some risks, and they can get you thinking. However, note that some sell-side reports will still outline things that might make the stock go down, even if they have a sell rating on the company. This will not be helpful if you are building the case for a short.

How to Handle Risks during the Interview

You don't have to actually mention the risks in your stock pitch. However, your interviewer might ask you about them and you should have an answer. If, however, one of your risks is a glaring, burning issue, then you should mention it, and then talk about why it has not prevented you from putting a buy on a stock.

As an example, if you are pitching a company as a buy when it has just had a well-publicized product recall, you might say something like "I've told you why I like the company. One of the key risks to investing in the stock is the recent product recall which has temporarily damaged the company's brand and reputation for safety. However, I believe that this is more than reflected in the recent stock price decline and the current very low valuation that the company is receiving; moreover, I believe that the management team is going to address the problem quickly and effectively, and rebuild trust with the consumer".

This is just an example, but I hope it gives you an idea of what I mean.

What are some other risks? I've listed some examples for my stock, Colgate. Please think of the ones that are appropriate for your company.

Risks for Colgate

Key risks for investing in Colgate include:

- Higher raw material costs could hurt the company's margins
- Increased competition could force the company to lower prices and impact its profitability. P&G is a particular threat in the oral care market.
- Increased competition from private label products
- The company has 75% of its sales outside the U.S., so currency movements, particularly a strong US dollar could negatively affect its sales and profits
- An economic slowdown would affect volumes, especially in some of the emerging markets

Think about Catalysts

Think about some events that could occur over the next few weeks or months that could cause the stock of your company to move. These are called catalysts.

There is no guarantee that these events will actually happen, of course, but it is still a good idea to try to identify a few things that could change investors' opinion of your stock, and cause them to bid the shares up (or down).

If you are building a buy (long) case you want to focus on things that could make the stock go up. If you are building a sell (short) case, you want to find events that could make the stock go down.

Catalysts can help to answer the question of "Why this stock now?" which is an important one for analysts to consider. With hundreds of publicly traded companies out there, many of them quite high in quality, you need to demonstrate why this particular stock should be owned at this point in time.

However, the importance of catalysts varies with the investment time horizon that is relevant for the asset manager who might hold the stock. So if, for example, you are interviewing with a short-term hedge fund that only has a 1-month investment time horizon, it will be very important to show that you have thought about events that could get the stock moving. On the other extreme, if you are interviewing with a value fund that has an average 3-5 year holding period for their stocks, then catalysts are much less relevant. In fact, you might not want to mention them at all, because it might make you seem too short-term in your outlook. Once again, it pays to do some research on a company before you step into a room to interview with one of its representatives.

As you will probably be using the same few stocks to interview with many different companies, it is a good idea to think of some catalysts for each stock, and use them when appropriate.

A good way to use the same stock for both long-term and short-term investment firms is to find a company that has a solid long-term thesis that you can always use, but also come up with a few short-term catalysts that are likely to get the stock moving soon.

Potential stock catalysts include (I am moving away from Colgate here so I can give a wide range of examples):

- The launch of a new product
- An acquisition or divestiture
- A stock buyback
- Management change
- In the next quarterly earnings release, the company will report earnings that are much better than the market expects (*but this can be hard to prove, so be careful*)

- Change in regulation
- Increase in orders
- Improvement in margins

These are just a few examples; there are many other potential ones.

If you are really having a hard time thinking of catalysts, then you can use something a bit more generic. You can even say that you don't have a specific catalyst, but you just believe that, "the company's strong earnings growth and consistent operating performance will cause its shares to be re-valued over time"; or that investors will, "reward the company if it does deliver on its margin targets, which you strongly believe it will do". Something like that.

Create a Document that Contains Your Entire Stock Pitch

Now that you have thought about all the main elements of your stock pitch, you should write them down in a document, along with a brief description of the industry or industries the company participates in, and what the company does (its main products and services). You may also want to include a chart of the stock price so you can see how it has performed recently and historically.

Please note that you should not take this document out during your actual interview. You will be expected to pitch the stock verbally without referring to anything written.

Don't Trust Your Memory

I would strongly advise that you do not trust what you have done to memory. Write it all down, preferably in an electronic format (e.g. MS Word). The advantage of this is that you can continue to refine your pitch as time goes by. You may come back from a few interviews and realize that you could phrase your arguments differently, or maybe add or subtract a point from your thesis. Maybe an interviewer brought up a risk that somehow you didn't think of. You can then add it to your risk section.

Add a Company Description

Adding a brief description of what the company does is helpful for jogging your memory if some time goes by between interviews. In addition, you may want to start off your pitch with this brief description, along with the market capitalization of the company, and the country in which it is based. Some companies, like Colgate, are easy to understand, and everyone may know about them. So Colgate might only need two lines of description. It might be useful to list some of the brands the company makes, since though everyone knows about its toothpaste, they may not realize that the company is also responsible for the Mennen, Speedstick, Irish Spring, and Ajax brands as well.

If your company is somewhat complicated and not very well-known, you will need to spend a bit of time explaining what it does. If it takes you more than two minutes to describe the company, you might want to choose something simpler.

Know the Market Cap

You should know the market capitalization of your company, also commonly called the "size" of the company. This is its number of shares outstanding times the current share price, and it is a number that is displayed with almost any quotation of the stock on sites like Yahoo Finance or Google Finance. Another useful number to have in your head is the approximate annual sales or revenues of the company, easily found on its income statement.

Congrats on Completing the Pitch!

So now you have completed your stock pitch. It was probably quite a time-consuming process, but it is a must when you are interviewing for equity research positions. Congratulations!

There are still a few other steps you need to take, however, to be fully prepared for your interviews.

Practise Out Loud

I would advise you to now take your written stock pitch and practise giving it out loud over and over again until you can do it well. You may want to have someone else listen to you and give you feedback.

It might also help you to listen to the stock pitches of others, especially professionals. If you watch TV channels like CNBC or Bloomberg TV, you will see that they quite frequently interview analysts (mainly from the sell-side) and fund managers to ask them about the stocks that they cover or are invested in. You can pick up a few tips from listening to the way they speak; watching the way they present themselves; and seeing how they handle questions.

Prepare to Defend Your Idea

You must prepare to defend your idea. It is quite likely that your interviewer will ask you one or two questions after you have presented your stock. The best outcome is that you have done your pitch convincingly and well, the interviewer has no major problems with what you have said, and just has a few questions that you can answer quite easily.

The worst case is that the interviewer violently disagrees with your analysis. There is not much you can do in that case except be prepared to defend what you have done.

You have to strike a balance between acknowledging the other person's views, and then explaining why you think you are right.

Don't Be Surprised by Different Views

Note that almost every stock that is trading is the subject of some debate. There will be some people who think it is a good buy, others who are neutral, and some who think it should not be touched. The sum total of these opinions is reflected in the current stock price of the company in the market. When you say that a company is a buy, you are essentially stating that the market is wrong, and that it should be trading at a higher price. So don't be surprised or offended if there is someone who disagrees with your view. The onus is actually on you to prove that the market is wrong. That's what your stock pitch is all about.

Note also that your interviewer doesn't have to share the same view as you on the stock to be impressed by your arguments. I remember someone who went into an interview and said that a stock was a sell. It turned out that the company he was interviewing with had a large holding in that company, i.e. they clearly thought it was a buy. However, they did not hold that against him, and he was invited back for another round of interviews. The point is, he presented his argument well, and they were impressed.

The less experienced you are, the less likely you are to get a lot of push-back on your idea, I think. If you are a student with no previous equity research experience, your interviewer might just be impressed that you were able to put together a coherent stock pitch. If you are an experienced analyst, however, expectations will be higher. Either way, you should be well-prepared. You never know when you are going to get a really tough interviewer, or someone who has had a bad morning, and decides to take it out on you by giving you a really hard time.

Have Conviction

Something you need to keep in mind when presenting your stock idea, and in fact, throughout your career as an equity analyst, is that you must have one essential quality: Conviction.

Conviction is very important when you are an analyst. You can't be lukewarm about your stock. You have to be really convinced that it is a buy (or a sell). You can't give up on your idea the moment someone presents you with a different opinion about the company. If you do, you will lose a lot of respect in the eyes of your interviewer.

Why is this quality so important? Well, think about it. In the real world, when working as an analyst, your recommendations, if followed, will result in a lot of money being invested in the markets. Depending on the size of the funds that the portfolio managers you are working with run, this could be millions of dollars. In addition to the responsibility of committing someone else's money to work, the portfolio managers are also putting their reputations on the line, since they are judged by the performance of their portfolios. So every time they buy or sell a stock, it is a meaningful decision that needs to be made carefully. They are looking to the analysts to help them make these decisions. In fact, as an analyst, you often have to persuade your fund managers to buy your stocks, to convince them that this is the right thing to do. But if you are wishy-washy on the idea, then you will never be able to pull that off. Why should they risk their clients' money and their careers if you don't even have the conviction to stand behind your own stock recommendation?

How to Prepare Your Defence

So, in order to prepare to defend your idea, I suggest you do some of the following:

- Think of challenges to your thesis. For example, if you say that you like that your company is launching several new products, a challenge could be that the last product the company launched was not successful, and that the current ventures might also be huge wastes of money
- Think of challenges that might arise from some of the risks you identified
- Think of challenges that could be brought against your valuation methodology or the numbers you have used
- Then think about answers you could give to each of these challenges that strike the right balance between humility and arrogance. You need to acknowledge the question, but give a confident response that shows your conviction in the idea

- Write down each challenge and its corresponding answer

- Practise answering each challenge out loud, as you did with your stock pitch

It is important to know the other side of the argument when you are pitching a stock. Coming up with these challenges will help you to do that. But you must not lose sight of your view, and thinking ahead of answers is a good exercise.

What if You Have No Answer to a Challenge?

Of course, it might happen that your interviewer challenges you on something that you have never even thought about, or that you didn't even know was an issue for the company. Hopefully you have done enough research so that this doesn't happen, but there is always going to be someone out there who knows much more about a stock than you do. You might be unlucky and get into an interview with that person.

In that case, what can you do?

Well, no matter how well you prepare, you have to be able to think quickly on your feet. So you might be able to come up with an effective counter-argument on the spot.

Another perfectly valid option is to just say "I don't know". You might have to admit that you hadn't factored that particular issue into your analysis, and that you might have to re-evaluate your opinion on your stock in the light of this new information. Don't feel pressed to change your opinion then and there, say you would need to think about it (unless your interviewer demands an immediate decision).

Hopefully, your challenges and corresponding responses will go a bit more like the ones I give in my example Colgate stock pitch interview session below.

Example Colgate Stock Pitch During an Interview

I am now going to give you an example of how I might pitch CL in an interview. I also give some example challenges from an interviewer, and potential responses to them. Hopefully, this will help to pull together most of the ideas I have presented in Chapter 4(II).

Please note that the pitch is at a business school level, i.e. it assumes that I have enough knowledge to do a valuation.

Interviewer:
What stock would you buy today?

Me:

I would buy Colgate-Palmolive. It is a global consumer products company that manufactures oral care, personal care, home care, and pet nutrition products. It is based in the US and has a market cap of about $40 billion dollars. Some of its major brands include Colgate, Speedstick and Irish Spring.

I like the company for a few reasons:

- First, Colgate has dominant market shares in toothpaste in some of the most important developing countries, including the BRICs: Brazil, Russia, India, and China. This represents a tremendous growth opportunity for the country as per capita toothpaste consumption is very low in many emerging countries. As these economies develop and incomes rise, more will be spent on consumer products.

- Secondly, the company is an extremely strong operator. It managed to grow earnings even during the recent global recession. It continues to steadily increase margins, and improve returns. It is a reliable cash generator. I believe that the market will continue to reward Colgate for its consistency of earnings.

- And finally, Colgate continues to focus on innovation, which is key for a consumer products company. It recently brought out two successful new oral care products, and I believe that this focus will continue to drive the company forward in the future.

In terms of valuation, I think the stock is attractive. It is trading on a p/e of about 16x, compared with its historical range of 18-30x. If the stock were to trade on the low end of the range, at 19x 2011 expected earnings, it would be worth $102, which would give 21% upside from the current stock price of $84.

I think the main catalyst will come from the reacceleration of revenue growth in 2010. Revenue growth was 0% in 2009. However, the emerging markets make up almost 50% of the company's sales, and those economies are rebounding quickly.

The company is also launching a few new products in 2010, and their success could get people excited about the stock.

Interviewer:

Don't you think that competition from private label is going to gradually erode the profitability of branded goods companies like Colgate?

Me:

Well, private label is a challenge for all branded companies. However, it has not had much success in Colgate's main toothpaste segment, with less than 1% market share.

I think this is because of the strength of Colgate's brand, and because toothpaste is too important a product to consumers for them to go with anything but a name they trust.

I don't see this changing in the future.

Interviewer:

What are some of the other key risks to the story?

Me:

Increased competition from P&G in the oral care market is a risk. However, Colgate has been successful in defending its market position before. The Venezuelan devaluation will hit the company, but it has already estimated the impact at 6-10 cents in 2010, only 1-2% of 2010's expected earnings. Also, the company's pet nutrition business is struggling a bit at the moment, but I believe that management will be able to turn it around soon.

Interviewer:

19x earnings isn't cheap. How is the stock trading relative to its peers?

Me:

Colgate is trading at a small premium to its consumer products peers like Procter & Gamble and General Mills. However, I think this is fully justified, as the company has better growth and stronger profitability. At 16x earnings, it is actually trading below the low end of its 10-year historical range of 18-30 times. I think the market has been worried about the impact of Venezuela, potential disruptions in other emerging markets, and its pet nutrition business. However, as revenue growth returns in 2010 and the company manages through these other issues, I think the valuation can rebound to its historical norms.

Interviewer:

How did margins hold up during the recession?

Me:

They held up quite well, in fact they improved. The operating margin held around 20% in 2007 and 2008 and improved to over 23% in 2009. Colgate was able to increase prices in 2009, and also controlled costs well. The company will also have benefited from lower raw material costs.

Interviewer:

Okay, good. So do you have any questions for me?

Chapter 4
Section (iii)

Understand and Prepare for Case and Brainteaser Interviews

Case and brainteaser questions are more common for undergraduate students than for business school students and experienced hires, in my experience.

Since asset management and sell-side firms are often open to hiring people who have non-finance or non-technical degrees, brainteaser questions are used as a way to check that the candidates have at least some of the quantitative skills that are necessary to do an equity research job. Hedge funds seem to particularly like using them. Case questions are used to test logic, analytical ability, and basic knowledge of how companies work, and what drives their profitability.

Business school students are more likely to encounter the stock pitch interview and its cousins, the stock presentation and "analyze a stock on the day" interviews. They are found in chapters 4(II), 4(V), and 4(VI). That being said, I have encountered a few case questions when interviewing for the sell-side, so it might be worth it to be prepared, just in case.

Case interviews are very common in management consulting, so if you have friends or classmates who are looking into this career path, you could swap notes with them, and maybe do a few practice cases.

There are two main types of case interviews: Number Estimation Cases and Business Cases.

Number Estimation Cases

A typical estimation case interview question would be something like the following:

How would you estimate the number of blue cars in the United States?

This is just an example. You could be asked to estimate the number of red cars, or burgers eaten every year, or suits bought, or whatever. And it might not be the United States; it could be Europe, Asia, Spain, the United Kingdom, anywhere. You get the idea.

The important thing to note is that your interviewer is generally not really concerned about whether or not you get to the right answer. In fact, they may not even know what the right answer is. What they do want to see is your thought process, and whether you can logically break a problem into parts, make sensible estimates about things, and do some basic math calculations.

Generally it is better if you can do all of the calculations in your head, but if you get a really complicated problem, with lots of parts that you have to estimate and then multiply or add together, don't be ashamed to pull out a piece of paper and write a few things down.

What you should not do is go silent, think for a long time, and then come up with an answer. Even if your answer is right, this does not help your interviewer. You need to talk through the process and let them see your mind working in action.

So, let's go through the" blue cars in the U.S." example. You might say something like the following:

- There are approximately 300 million people in the United States
- I estimate that there are 3 people per household, so that means there are 100 million households
- Let's assume that 60% of these households own a car. That may seem low, but remember that there will always be a percentage of the population that doesn't own cars: students, the very elderly, people in big cities where public transportation is abundant and owning a car is expensive and a hassle, etc.
- So that means there are 60 million cars in the U.S.
- What percentage is blue? Well, I don't think blue is a particularly popular colour choice for cars in the U.S. I would estimate that only 5% of cars are blue.
- 5% of 60 million is 3 million
- So I estimate there are 3 million blue cars in the U.S.[3]

---

[3] For those of you that are interested, according to Wikipedia, there were 251 million registered passenger vehicles in the U.S. in 2006, of which 135 million were classified as automobiles (the rest were trucks, SUVs, etc). So my 60 million was way off. That being said, it was off by less than 1 order of magnitude.

Note that every single one of my assumptions could be wrong (well, except for the 300 million people and 3 people per household). But maybe 80% of households own a car, and maybe 15% of them are blue. That would change my answer dramatically. But that is not the point. The point is that I showed that I could break the problem down, make some reasonable estimates, and do some simple maths to come up with an answer.

The only way to really prepare for this is to make up a few cases and practise thinking about how you might answer them. You should also probably know a few key facts about your country or region, and some of the major countries and regions of the world (like the populations of the U.S., EU zone, China, etc). You might also want to know the sizes of their economies.

Then when you are posed a question like the one above in an interview, try to keep calm, and think logically about how you might break the problem down.

Business Cases

Business cases involve analyzing companies and some of the real-world problems or issues they may face. They could involve asking you to think about how a particular company might be valued or what the drivers of that valuation would be, even if you are not asked to come up with an actual number.

The case will typically start off by you being asking a rather open-ended question. A discussion will then ensue between you and your interviewer about this problem. You might be given additional information as the case goes on, or asked to evaluate alternative scenarios. Your interviewer will be observing your creativity, analytical ability, and judgement. Your communication skills will also be on display. Can you deal with new and unexpected data? How well do you handle pressure? Are you articulate and confident?

There is an extremely wide range of case questions you could be asked, but I have listed a few examples to get you thinking:

- An ice-cream shop opens up on your street. After running for a year it has opened up 2 more stores in your town. One of your friends decides that he wants to buy the entire operation and asks for your advice. How would you go about evaluating the company's prospects and deciding how much your friend should be willing to pay for it?

- A high end consumer products company based in Europe is considering entering the Chinese market. What issues should the company consider before making this decision?

- A company that sells drugs and healthcare supplies to hospitals suddenly starts losing money after years of operating profitably. How would you figure out the problem, and what advice would you give to the company?

- A utility company is considering investing in various power generation sources: coal, natural gas, nuclear, and wind. What should they consider when deciding the best mix?

Because there is such a variety in what you could be asked, you will need to be able to think on your feet. That being said, there are certain principles that will underlie every case. All businesses consist of revenue and costs, and the difference between them is profits. Revenues, in turn, consist of units sold (or the applicable metric in a service industry) and pricing. Therefore, when you are answering a case question, try to frame it around these issues: units, pricing, revenue, costs and profits. You will need to take into account all of the different factors that could impact these drivers including the all-important issue of competition. If you need more information on the drivers of business performance, please consult some of the resources in the Appendix. *Competitive Strategy* by Michael Porter should be particularly helpful.

Brainteasers

Brainteaser interviews are perhaps even harder to prepare for because you could be asked almost anything. Examples might include mathematical calculations that you are expected to do in your head or logic puzzles:

- What is 3/7 expressed as a decimal?
- What is 10^3 times 10^7?
- It is 3 o'clock. How many degrees are there between the hands on a circular clock?
- Why are manhole covers round?

Probably the best way to prepare is to practice answering a few questions of this type so that you are not completely at a loss if you are given one in an interview. Look up "brain teasers" on the internet and try answering a few. Be well rested on the day of the interview so that you can think quickly.

Other Technical Questions

Finally, note that business school students and experienced candidates may get technical questions about finance, valuation, or accounting, because they will be expected to know the answers. Undergrad students who have degrees in business or finance may also be tested. All you can do is make sure that you have a good grasp of these subject matters so that you are well-prepared to answer any question that may be thrown at you.

Chapter 4
Section (iv)

Understand and Prepare for the
Hostile Interview

I am classifying a hostile interview as one in which you are asked questions that make you uncomfortable or annoyed. It is unlikely that an entire interview will be made up of questions of this type, but you could get a few of them, interspersed with more typical challenges like, "Tell me a stock that you like at the moment".

Luckily, hostile interviews are not very common on the buy side, at least judging from my experience. But I have had a couple of them, so it pays to be prepared.

In addition to the questions you are asked, the setting could appear hostile or intimidating. For example, you might find that you are on one side of a table with ten people opposite you, each firing questions at you in turn. I don't actually mind this situation that much if the questions are fair. Nevertheless, it could be rather nerve-racking for some people.

Why the Hostile Interview?

Why would I be given a hostile interview, you might ask? What would be the motivation of my interviewer?

It could be that it is a test to see how well you handle pressure. Or the answer could be that your interviewer doesn't intend to be hostile, he or she just has a few genuine concerns about your CV and needs some questions answered. On the other hand, the person interviewing you might really be an insensitive and unpleasant person who likes making other people feel bad (unfortunately, there are people like that, even in equity research). Regardless of the reason, you need to be prepared.

Potential Questions

Here are some of the "hostile" questions you might be faced with:

- Why aren't your grades better?
- Why should I hire someone as inexperienced as you?
- You were made redundant at your previous job: is there something wrong with you?
- What makes you so special?

How do you deal with this?

Well, you need to take pre-emptive action.

Sit down before you start interviewing and think about anything that might represent a weakness or gap in your academic record, experience, or CV. Be honest and try to be objective. Maybe ask a trusted friend to help you with this exercise (but only if you won't hold it against this person afterwards!)

Now, if you've read everything that I've written before, I am sure you know what is coming: think of appropriate responses to these concerns, write them down, and then practice your answers out loud. Potentially use your friend to critique your answers. Otherwise, just say them to yourself, over and over, until you like how it sounds.

The Right Response

That is all very well, but what are the right responses to give, you may ask? That is a bit difficult to answer because there will be as many responses as there are potential questions, and I can't anticipate what all of them will be. But I've written a few examples below that should help you as you think about your particular situation.

Why are your undergraduate grades so low?

- My undergraduate grades were a bit disappointing, but I scored an impressive 790 on my GMAT. I think this proves that I am in the top decile of my peers.

OR

- My overall GPA is not very high. However, if you look at my finance and accounting courses, I got straight As.

You have no previous research, finance, or accounting experience. Why on earth should I hire you?

- I have a computer science degree and before business school I worked as an engineer. This means that I have very strong analytical skills and I am extremely comfortable with numbers. These are very important attributes for an equity analyst to have. In addition, I am taking several advanced finance courses in my second year of business school.

Why were you laid off from your previous job? Is there something wrong with you?

- Because of the credit crisis and the way it affected my previous employer's parent company, my whole division was made redundant. Unfortunately, even though my team and I had very strong performance, we were still affected by this corporate decision.

Arguing with Everything You Say

Another type of "hostile" interview you might encounter is one in which your interviewer is intentionally argumentative, disagreeing with everything you say, or taking the other side of every argument that you put forward. The person may be doing this mainly to see how you react. In some ways, this is not bad preparation for life as an equity research analyst because analysts are often called upon to defend their ideas and stock calls in the face of scepticism from others.

How to Act during the Interview

During the interview itself, if you are faced with an obnoxious question, it is important to stay calm. Keep your cool, and try not to get defensive. Remember, this is just an interview; it is not life and death (though it may feel like that sometimes, I know!) As much as possible, don't let your interviewer know that you have become uncomfortable or annoyed. Pause, smile, and then rattle off the answer you have prepared, in a confident and professional manner.

It is always harder to respond well if you are caught by surprise. But if you have anticipated a difficult question and prepared for it, you will come out on top.

Of course, if you are asked something really inappropriate, you can refuse to answer.

Chapter 4
Section (v)

Understand and Prepare for the
Stock Presentation Interview

The stock presentation is quite a typical interview type. It is closely related to the stock pitch interview. The main difference is that you are expected to present the stock in written rather than verbal form. And the presentation is usually expected to be longer and more detailed than your typical stock pitch.

Stock presentations are rarely used in a first round of interviews. They tend to come in the second or later rounds, and they can be a key differentiator between candidates.

The format is that you are either given a stock by the company you are interviewing with or you are told to choose one yourself. You are given a certain amount of time to research the stock, and this could be anywhere from a week to a month. You are then expected to come back with a presentation on the company, and an opinion on what you would do with the shares today, i.e. whether the stock is a buy or a sell. You will typically be asked to make your presentation to a small group of people, and you will be asked questions either during your presentation or after it. The questions could be about anything related to your presentation – the industries the company operates in, what the company does, its financial performance, your valuation methodology, etc.

I will go through how this should be approached shortly, but first, I would like to give you my number 1 tip for this interview type:

Put In a Lot of Effort

Put a **lot** of time and effort into your presentation. Typically, you will not be given much guidance on what it is supposed to look like. You may only be told, for example, that you have 30-45 minutes to present the stock. Theoretically, you could just hand out a simple sheet of paper with a few bullet points that get your main ideas across. My advice is not to do this. Go all out. Put as much time, effort, and care into the presentation as you can. It is almost impossible to impress your interviewers so much that they don't want to hire you. It is very possible, and quite easy, however, to underwhelm someone. If you put a lot of effort into something, it will show, and you will do much better than most of your competitors. This will significantly raise your chances of getting hired.

I know this works because on two occasions, after I slaved over a stock presentation for days on end, I was complimented about them by the people I subsequently presented them to. In one case it was the final interview, and I got a job offer. The head hunter who was involved with the search actually told me that my presentation was the deciding factor. In the other instance I was told several times how impressive my presentation was, and I was brought through to the next round of interviews.

Key Steps in Creating the Presentation

Here are the key steps you should take when you are preparing your stock presentation:

- Do the research on the stock.

- Decide whether it is a buy or a sell. Preferably it should be one of these two ratings. If you are given a stock (rather than allowed to choose one yourself) you might find that you really can't argue anything but a hold. But if you can make it a buy or a sell then that's better, because it allows you to show more conviction. No wimpy "outperform" or "underperform" or "market perform" ratings, please. Buy, Sell, or if you must, Hold. That's it.

- Write your presentation. Don't leave this for the last minute. It should actually be given at least as much of your preparation time as steps 1 and 2, because it can take a very long time to put a good presentation together.

- Practise, practise, and practise your presentation. Don't read silently to yourself, no, practise out loud, over and over. Do this until you can give the presentation fluently and with assurance. You might want to get someone to listen to you and give you feedback. Also please time yourself so that you are not taking 60 minutes

103

when you have been given a 30 minute time slot. If you are, you need to either speed up your presentation or, more likely, cut some pages out. A good rule of thumb is that you should budget 1 minute for each slide in your presentation. Note that if you don't know how much time you have to present, you should ask the company in advance. Don't guess.

- Anticipate the questions you might get and have answers for them.

- Make the requested number of copies plus a few extras in case additional people turn up, and make sure to bring them with you. If you don't know how many to bring, ask your interviewer.

- I like to have a copy of the presentation that I keep for myself, that I will mark with notes, cues and reminders that will help me to give the presentation and answer questions. I also like to have a copy of some of the key back-up data so that I can refer to them if I get asked a question I can't answer from memory. They would include the company's financial statements, any model I've built, and my valuation analysis. Bring whatever you think you might need.

- If you are very nervous about giving presentations or need additional help with the actual speech and delivery part of it, you may want to seek out some help or even coaching. Your career office might be able to help you with this, and there are many books and resources on the topic.

Refer to the Stock Pitch Chapter, 4(II)

For help on the first step, doing the research on the stock, please refer to Chapter 4(II): Understand and Prepare for the Stock Pitch Interview. In this chapter I go through how to pitch a stock, and the main component of this is doing the research and valuation. This is exactly what you have to do for your stock presentation.

If you are an undergraduate student with a non business-related degree and you are asked to do a stock presentation, try to find out what is required of you in the area of financial analysis and valuation. Your interviewers know that you don't have the background in these disciplines, and it is unlikely that you will be expected to do much. You should therefore adjust the advice I give in the rest of this chapter with that in mind.

You May Not Get to Choose the Stock

One difference from the stock pitch is that you are likely to be given the stock by the company you are interviewing with. So unfortunately, it may be in a sector that you are not familiar with or do not particularly like. But you need to overcome this and do the best you can on the research.

Show Conviction

Whatever you decide, whether it is a buy or a sell, as I mentioned in Chapter 4(II), you need to show conviction. If it is a hold, maybe because there isn't enough upside in the valuation, think about at what level you would buy or sell the stock. And try to show the conviction of your beliefs in other parts of your presentation e.g. have a definite view about the industry, the company, its performance, management, etc.

Leave Time to Write

In step 3 you have to actually write the presentation. There are many ways to do this, of course. If you have written presentations in the past, and you have a proven format, please go with that.

If you need some guidance, I give an example format below. Feel free to modify it as it makes sense for you. You can also vary the number of slides in each section to make sure your presentation is not too long or too short.

I like to use Microsoft PowerPoint or Word. Word can actually be made to look like a power point presentation if you use it in landscape mode.

Example Stock Presentation Format

Title Page

Put the name and ticker of the stock you are presenting as well as your name.

Agenda

Give a list of the main topics to be covered in the presentation. In this case it is:

- Thesis and Recommendation
- Company Description
- Expansion of Thesis
- Valuation
- Key Risks
- Potential Catalysts
- Summary

The agenda page should only be one page long.

Thesis and Recommendation

Give your recommendation on the stock (e.g. buy/sell), current price, valuation/target price, and upside.

Outline the thesis in bullet points.

Try to get this all on one page of the presentation.

Company Description

Even if the company was given to you by your interviewers, don't assume that everyone in the audience knows what it does. So give a description of the company.

Depending on how complicated the company is - this could take a couple of pages or several. You might want to use graphs and tables to illustrate key data.

Here is some information you might want to include in this section:

- Key business segments and their percentage of revenues and/or profits of the company
- Geographical breakdown of revenues
- Porter's 5 forces of industry attractiveness for the businesses the company is involved in
- Market capitalization and annual revenues
- Operating margin of each segment
- 5 year history of key company financial metrics such as sales growth, operating margin, earnings growth, leverage ratios, ROIC, etc. A table is useful for summarizing this.
- Graph of the company's share price performance, absolute and/or relative to the market

Expansion of Thesis

This is the real meat of the presentation, and can be as long or as short as you want it.

You might want to take 1-2 slides to go into more detail about each point in the thesis. Hopefully you only have 3-5 points.

You can use graphs, charts, tables or just text to back-up and explain each point. I would advise having a few graphs, if possible. They can sometimes illustrate a point with much more clarity than lines and lines of text. And they can make your presentation seem more analytical, more data and numbers-driven. Analysts and fund managers tend to like that, and they are likely to be your primary audience. That being said - don't throw in a pointless graph just for the sake of it. Use them only when it makes sense.

Don't be afraid to inject your opinion into the thesis. It shouldn't just be a lot of data. Any set of data has to be interpreted, and different people can look at the same raw information and come up with different conclusions. The point is, this is your presentation, and you are giving your view on the stock.

Valuation

Here you outline how you did the valuation and came up with your target price.

If you built a company model and a DCF, you could list the key variables like the terminal growth rate and WACC. If you feel comfortable doing so, you could list all your main model assumptions in a table e.g. revenue growth rate, margins, free cash flow, etc. However, if you do that, make sure you are prepared to explain each one. Another strategy is to keep this out of the presentation, but have the information in your back-up pack, in case someone asks.

If you are arguing that the company is cheaper than its peers, you could have a table which has the p/e ratios of your company and a few of its main competitors.

Even though the valuation is a key element of your stock analysis, it probably doesn't need to take up more than 1-3 pages in your presentation.

Key Risks

List the main risks that could affect your company and its stock price.

Please note that I also went through how to do this in the Stock Pitch chapter (Chapter 4(II)).

Be prepared to discuss these risks and why they are not big enough to put you off owning (or shorting) the stock.

Potential Catalysts

List a few events that could occur over the next few weeks or months and get the stock moving.

Again, this was covered in the Stock Pitch chapter.

Summary

This is optional and can be skipped if you are running out of time. However, I think it is useful to have one page at the end that summarizes your whole presentation. It could look quite a lot like your Thesis and Recommendation page, though maybe with a bit more colour thrown in.

Or you could choose to pare things down and make a few bold statements like "I would buy this stock now" or "I believe this is a stock that should be held by investors with a medium to long-term time frame" or "I'd short this stock today. It is a disaster waiting to happen" or "This is a stock to own, but it is not for the faint of heart".

Write whatever seems appropriate now that you are at the end of your presentation.

Chapter 4
Section (vi)

Understand and Prepare for the
"Analyze a Stock on the Day" Interview

This is one of the toughest types of interview you will encounter when looking for equity research jobs. It is not as common as the stock pitch or the stock presentation interviews, but it is not atypical either.

The format is that on the day of the interview itself, you are given a company that you have to analyze and present that very day. You will be given information about the company (typically its financial statements, annual reports, stock price data, etc) and a certain amount of time, likely 1-3 hours. After your time is up, you will be expected to present your views on the company and/or the stock to a person or group of people. There will often be a question and answer session after your presentation (they ask the questions, you answer).

This is tough because doing research on a company, analyzing its financial statements, coming up with a valuation and deciding on a rating (buy or sell) is an activity that can sometimes take experienced analysts days or even weeks to do. So attempting to do the same in 2 hours can be a rather daunting task.

Hopefully, you will be given some clear guidelines on what you will be expected to present. For example, you may be charged with coming up with 5 or 6 key questions that you would ask the management of the company. Unfortunately, you may instead be given a very vague mandate like "just tell us what you think about the company".

Below are my key tips for dealing with this type of interview.

Try to Get a Clear Understanding of What You Are Supposed to Do

As I mentioned, sometimes you will be given a very clear mandate e.g. "Please analyze this company for the next 3 hours. At the end of it, we would like to know the 5-6 issues you would bring up if you had an interview with the management team".

If you are given very clear instructions like this, then that's great, you can focus your time on making sure you follow them to the best of your ability.

However, if you are given a very vague mandate like, "When we come back we'd just like to have a discussion about the company", then really try to push for more information before you are left alone to do your analysis. An open-ended assignment like this is very difficult to manage, and you will reduce your chances of failure a lot if you can get some more guidance.

What to Do if No Guidance is Given

If your interviewer refuses to be more specific, however, I would try to answer the following questions. They should prepare you for most discussions about the company:

- Is this a company that is doing well or poorly financially?
- What do I think about the industry or industries the company is operating in?
- What do I think about the strategic plans and goals the management team has set out for the company?
- What are the main questions I would ask the management of the company if I had an interview with them?
- What valuation would I give to this company?
- Would I buy or sell the stock?

Have a Buy/Sell Decision

In fact, if you are given the data to do so, I would try to come up with answers to the last two questions even if not explicitly asked to. This is because, at the end of the day, answering those two questions is the main job of an equity analyst. So be prepared to give an answer, even if it involves doing a very quick and not-very-detailed valuation analysis and going with your gut feel about the company.

The exception is if you are an undergraduate student with a non business-related degree. If you are given an interview of this type, the company will know that you don't have the knowledge to do a valuation, and so it is unlikely that you will be expected to comment on it. You should also adjust the advice I give in the rest of this chapter with that in mind.

Leave 5-10 Minutes at the End to Prepare What You Are Going to Say

This is probably my number 1 tip for this type of interview.

It is tempting to spend all of the limited time you have pouring through the company's annual reports and financial statements, trying to decide what you think about the stock, and answering the questions you were given. However, it is no use doing all of this analysis if you present it poorly at the end. Your interviewers can only judge what they see and hear, they cannot give you credit for anything else. And you will be much more effective at presenting your conclusion if you have taken a few minutes to prepare what you are going to do beforehand.

So give yourself a hard deadline, and stop all of your analysis at that point. Decide what you are going to say. Write it down, and if possible, practise it a few times, maybe silently in your mind or in a low voice.

Have a Game Plan

It is unlikely that you will just show up for the interview and be told that you need to analyze a stock on the spot. You are likely to be told in advance about the interview format. Therefore you can prepare for it. True, you don't know what company you will be given, but that is no excuse for not preparing for the interview in other ways.

You can prepare by deciding in advance exactly how you are going to analyze the company once you are presented with all of its associated information.

Then once you are given the data on the company, you can get to work right away. You don't need to start wondering, at that point, what you should do next.

Of course, you might need to adjust your game plan a bit depending on exactly what you are asked to present. But being prepared will still put you at an advantage.

I would urge you to think of non-financial as well as financial areas for analysis. The financials are important, but they rarely give the complete picture. You interviewer may also want to know what you think about some of the broader issues around the firm.

A good idea is to read through and familiarize yourself with the typical structure of a few company reports before you go into the interview, so that you know where to look to find what you want.

Below are some key calculations and questions you may want to prepare and answer. Make sure you memorize some of the ratios, don't assume you can bring in a cheat sheet (I would not do that unless you are explicitly told you can). And of course, please add to (or subtract from) this list as you see fit.

Please note that the annual reports of some companies may have a page or two that already lists many of the key financial ratios below for several years. In that case, you don't have to re-calculate them.

Also note that you may only want to calculate some of these ratios at certain times and not at others. For instance, if you see that the company's operating margins are declining, you may want to delve in and see whether that was as a result of changes in the gross margin, SG&A/Sales or R&D/Sales, etc. If the margins are stable or increasing, however, you may not feel the need to go into this level of detail.

If you need more information about these ratios and other aspects of financial analysis, please see the resources listed in the Appendix. Otherwise, the textbooks used in your university or business school courses should be helpful. As I've mentioned, undergraduate students are unlikely to be expected to know about financial ratio analysis and valuation. However, the advice given about other matters will apply.

Financial ratios (calculate these for a few years as the data permits, so you can see trends)

- Sales growth
- Operating margin (or EBIT margin)
- Net margin
- SG&A/Sales
- R&D /Sales
- Net income growth
- Eps growth
- ROE
- ROIC
- Interest coverage
- Debt/Capitalization
- Net Debt/Capitalization

- Free cash flow
- Free cash flow/Net income

Also interesting to observe are the amounts spent on the following:

- Share buybacks
- Debt pay down
- Acquisitions

Industry

- Is the company operating in an attractive industry? *The margins and ROE can give you a clue if you don't know.*
- Does the industry seem to be getting more or less competitive? *The company may mention competition in its annual reports, or you may have knowledge of the industry.*
- How fast is the industry growing?
- How does this industry look under a Porter's 5 Force Analysis (barriers to entry, rivalry, buyer power, supplier power, substitutes)?

Company's Position

- How is the company positioned? Is it a leader? Is it an up and comer?
- Does it have a sustainable competitive advantage?
- What are its realistic growth opportunities?
- Is this a quality business?
- What are the key opportunities and challenges for the company?

Management

- What is management's strategic plan for the company?
- What are their stated goals?
- How have they typically used the free cash of the company (e.g. stock buybacks, acquisitions, paying down debt)?

Valuation

- What is the company worth?

Assume Your Interviewer Knows the Company Well

Your interviewers are likely to give you a company that they know well. It may be one whose stock they own or have owned in the past.

Keep this in mind, but don't let it intimidate you. You are entitled to your own opinion on the stock, even if it is diametrically opposed to theirs. Just be wary of the instinct to make things up or "B-S" your way out of a hard question – you are likely to get caught out. If you really have no clue about the answer to something, just say that you don't know.

Do Not Try to Read Everything

Most likely you will be given an annual report or several annual reports for the company. You may also be given quarterly earnings release data, charts, historical valuation data, and even sell-side reports.

The one thing you **do not** want to attempt to do is sit down and read everything you have been given and then start your analysis. If you do that, you are headed for complete disaster. Just reading one annual report is likely to take up all of your time.

You need to hunt for the data that you need. This is where having a game plan is essential (see earlier in this chapter).

You don't want to sit and read or aimlessly leaf through the data you have been given. You decide what you need to analyze or calculate, and then you go for it.

If you want the operating margin for the past 2 years – go to the income statements.

If you want the ROE – go to the income statement and the balance sheet. As I've mentioned previously, the company may have already calculated some ratios for you and placed them in a table in its annual report.

There are some things that you will need to read the text to find, however. If you want to know what management's strategic plans are for the company, and how it thinks it has performed over the previous year, you will need to read the beginning of the report or the Management Discussion section to find them.

As I've said previously, familiarize yourself with a few company reports before you go into the interview so that you know where to look to find what you want.

Don't Get Too Bogged Down in the Details

It is easy to get very bogged down in the details when you are analyzing a company. That's fine if you have a month to prepare, but not if you have 2-3 hours. If you find you are spending a lot of time digging through all the Notes to the Financial Statements or trying to figure out exactly why the company's tax rate is only 28.5% one year when it was 26.7% the year before, you have probably gone too far.

Take a step back and try to see the big picture. Is this a good company? Is it operating in an attractive industry? Would you buy the stock? And most importantly, are you getting any closer to answering the questions your interviewer asked you to answer about the company?

Of course, the numbers are very important, and if your opinion about the company does hinge on its tax rate, you should obviously analyze it in detail. But that is rarely the case.

Note Important Page Numbers

When you are reading through all the annual reports, financial statements, and other documents, you may find it helpful to note the page numbers of key data or information. That way, if you need to refer to them again, either later on in your analysis or during the Q&A session, you will be able to find them quickly.

Take Cues from Previous Interviews

This interview type is unlikely to be given in a first round, so you will probably have had at least one interview with the company before.

Use the information and feedback you have gathered from these meetings to help you during this interview, both during your analysis, and afterwards during your presentation and Q&A session.

For example, if the company you are interviewing with is very focused on balance sheet strength, then make sure you pay attention to leverage and liquidity ratios when you are analyzing your company, and address the balance sheet during your presentation.

Also pay attention to slightly softer issues. For example, you may have received feedback that the company is concerned that you might not be able to make decisions fast enough, because buy/sell calls have to be made very quickly with not a lot of information at the firm. In that case, make sure that you have a definite opinion on whether or not you would buy or sell the company's shares, even if you have been given very little time and not much information. That might be the point, to give you a test. I would also carefully evaluate whether or not that place is right for you. You might not feel comfortable with that speed of analysis, and maybe even find it irresponsible.

If Pushed, Be Opinionated

In my opinion, it isn't really realistic to have a definite buy/sell opinion on a stock after only being allowed to analyze it for 2-3 hours. Even if I know the industry the company is operating in pretty well, it would still take me more time, and I have been doing this for years.

I think there are some things you *can* figure out about a company in a couple of hours, however. Coming up with a few key questions for the management team makes sense to me. And it is possible to do a quick valuation analysis based on historical p/e ratios and earnings (if they are supplied), or other data of this sort. But to have a strong buy or sell rating is tough, I think.

Nevertheless, you may be pushed to give an opinion, and if so you should do it and do it with conviction. That is my advice for succeeding in this type interview. If someone asks you what you would do with the stock, it's because they think you should have an answer, and it won't serve you well if you waffle or hedge, even if that's actually the appropriate thing to do under the circumstances. Remember, people in this industry love conviction.

I am speaking from experience because I once failed an interview of this type. I wasn't given any stock price information, yet I was asked whether or not I would buy the company today. I didn't express a strong view, and was later told that I hadn't impressed the interviewers. They thought I should have been able to come down one way or another: yes I'd buy it, or no I wouldn't.

Chapter 4
Section (vii)

Expect Several Rounds of Interviews

I have used terms like "first round" and "second round" interviews throughout this book. Perhaps it is obvious what this means, but I will clarify briefly. When you have your first set of interviews with a company, whether it is one interview or three, it is referred to as your first round. If you are invited back as part of a smaller group of applicants that have passed the initial screening of the first round, you will have your second round of interviews. And so on.

Three Rounds is Typical

Almost without exception, there will be at least two rounds of interviews for any equity research job. Maybe there are summer placements that will make job offers after only one round of interviews, but generally, one round is a rare occurrence.

You may get an offer after two rounds of interviews, but three rounds is quite typical for most full-time equity research jobs, I would say. Some firms take it even further, to four or more rounds.

The Timing Can Vary

The time between interview rounds can vary. If you are graduating from university and meeting companies that come on campus, there is usually a predetermined and relatively fast-moving schedule that you will follow. The process probably won't take more than a few weeks.

If you are not a student, or you are a student who is applying to companies that have not come in search of you, or you are going through head hunters or a website job posting, the timing of the interview process can vary greatly. Some companies that have posted a position and need to fill it immediately might get all three rounds done within a month. Other times the process can be excruciatingly slow, taking several months. This may be because the decision-making process in the company takes a long time, or because the people who are supposed to interview you are very busy or travelling.

The Type of Interview to Expect in Each Round

Each round of interviews, even with the same company, may take on a different form.

The first round almost always involves a Resume/CV Review interview [Chapter 4(I)]. If you meet new people in subsequent rounds, they may ask you similar questions, so always be prepared for this interview type. You should also always be prepared for the hostile interview, just in case [Chapter 4(IV)].

Business school students should also come to the first interview with 1-2 stock pitches prepared [Chapter 4(II)]. As I mentioned previously, if you are interviewing with hedge funds, you should have at least 1 long idea and 1 short idea. Undergraduates may want to prepare a pared-down version of a stock pitch, as I described in that chapter.

If you are invited back for further rounds of interviews, you will usually be told in advance whether you are going to be asked to make a stock presentation that you have prepared, or whether you will be asked to analyze a stock on the day. Then you can consult the relevant chapters [4(V) and 4(VI)].

The Case and Brainteaser interviews [Chapter 4(III)] are more common for undergraduate students, so they should be prepared for them from the first round. Business school students may not want to spend too much time on them, but it doesn't hurt to be prepared just in case. So make sure you are aware of how to approach this type of interview in case you do encounter it.

Chapter 5

Key Interviewing Tips

In this chapter, I am going to share some of my key tips for the entire interviewing process. In the introduction to Chapter 4, I gave some practical interview preparation points, and there may be a few repeats here from that section, as well as from other parts of the book. But I also want to address some additional issues in this chapter, things that have to do with your attitude and overall approach to the job-hunting process.

Be Enthusiastic

Be enthusiastic when you interview for jobs. Try to approach the whole thing as an adventure, the beginning of an exciting new phase in your life, a thrilling new challenge. Your energy and enthusiasm will shine through during your interviews, and will be noticed by even the most hardened, world-weary portfolio manager. He or she may remain stony faced throughout your interview, but you can bet that some positive comments will be made about how enthusiastic you were when feedback is given about you. It is almost impossible to be too eager when you are looking for a job.

If you don't feel excited and upbeat about the whole thing, then try to pump yourself up before each interview. Do whatever works for you. A tired, dreary attitude will be noticed.

Please remember that no one owes you a job. No matter how accomplished, experienced, or all-round fantastic a person you may be, the onus is on you to convince a company to actually hire and pay you. It doesn't matter how great your business school or university is. Sure, that may get you through the door to the interview, but it certainly doesn't guarantee you a job offer.

Companies want enthusiastic, fired up employees. Don't act as though you are tired or bored or wish you were somewhere else during the interview. Even if you are not crazy about the prospect of working for a particular company, act as though you are. If you are taking up enough of your and their time to interview, you should be prepared to put in the proper amount of effort. The other point is that you are training yourself in the art of interviewing, and it is better to practise well each time, not half-heartedly.

Overall, be aware that when you are looking for a job, you have to get off your high horse. You may even have to "sing for your supper" for a bit. What I mean is that until you do get an offer with a company, the people at that company are the ones with the power, the control. They are in the driver's seat. And for as long as they see fit, you are going to have to do a bit of a song and dance for their pleasure: "Yes, I'd love to work at your company; Yes, I really want to work as an equity research analyst; Yes, I'm really enthusiastic about the job." If the company initially says there will only be two interview rounds, and then after the second round it tells you it has decided to add on three more rounds, you don't complain, you just suck it up and interview again.

I'm not saying to grovel, but you should be accommodative, be pleasant, and be responsive. Ask questions, be positive. Don't be disdainful or cynical.

You catch my drift.

Of course we all have different personalities, and you need to be yourself. All I'm saying is to be the most positive, enthusiastic version of yourself that you can be while you are interviewing.

The good news is that once you get a job offer, all the power reverts to you. You are then in the driver's seat as you can either reject the offer or accept it. And the company will really want you to accept its offer.

Be Confident

Be confident during your interviews. Remember, you are being judged on your interpersonal skills as well as your analytical abilities. Now, unlike other more client-facing roles (like the sell-side, corporate finance, or management consulting), you don't have to present an absolutely smooth corporate image. A bit more quirkiness, even weirdness, is tolerated on the buy side. Still, part of your job will be to convince people to follow your stock recommendations and commit real money to them, so you have to inspire confidence in others.

To do that you first need to have confidence in yourself.

So speak up, look at people directly, and don't be mousy.

As I mentioned in the chapter on preparing a stock pitch [Chapter 4 (II)], have conviction when you deliver your views on a stock. Take a stand, don't be wishy-washy.

Be very definite about your desire to do equity research. Speak emphatically about the issue if you are asked, and try to mention this even if you are not asked, i.e. weave it into the answer to another question if possible. Be able to express the reasons why you want to do the job.

Most of all, believe that you deserve to have this job. People can sense it if you don't. And if you have followed the guidelines in this book and done all the preparation I have advised, you will deserve the job (no one owes you a job, as I said before, but you do deserve one).

Don't Be Arrogant

Be confident, but don't let this turn into arrogance. There is a difference, and most of us know very well what it is.

Don't be rude. Don't be condescending.

Some people seem to think that this sort of behaviour is accepted or even expected in the world of finance. That may or may not be true at some companies, but it is not a good working assumption when you are trying to find a job.

Don't Get Discouraged by Rejection

When you are interviewing, it is inevitable that you will face some rejection along the way. Realize that this is a part of the process, and don't get discouraged by it.

Some companies will just not give you an interview, despite your brilliant resume and cover letter. Others will reject you after the first round. Even more heartbreakingly, you may be turned down at the very end of the process, after making it all the way to the final round. You need to accept that these things will happen, despite your best efforts. Some places are just not right for you, even though you think they are. Or sometimes there will be another candidate who is just that little bit better than you in the company's eyes. Chin up, carry on, and go to the next interview. If you keep interviewing, you are likely to get an offer eventually.

If you think it will help you, try to get feedback from companies on why you have been rejected after an interview. I would not advise that you hunt down the companies that did not even give you an interview. But if you have been turned down after an interview has taken place, especially in a later round, it is fine to call the company up afterwards and ask if you can get some feedback about what went wrong. Be pleasant about it, and don't argue. If they say you lacked enthusiasm about the role, yet you know you were really excited about it, the issue is yours, not theirs. You were obviously not communicating your feelings well. Make a mental note and adjust for the next interview.

Getting negative feedback can be tough sometimes, but curb the urge to lash out at the company, no matter how wrong you think they are. No good can come of that.

Be Persistent

Don't be afraid to push for the job you really want. Companies like to have employees that really want to work for them, and showing this enthusiasm and tenacity might just give you an extra edge.

When you are looking for a job, it can become front and centre of your mind, almost all day, every day. You may be tempted to think that the companies, head hunters, and HR people you are dealing with are in the same frame of mind. But you need to remember that they often have many other things going on. The people at the company have their main jobs to do, which involve research, travelling, managing portfolios, etc. Head hunters have other candidates and other positions to fill. The point is that you are the person who is most concerned about your career, and you need to drive it forward. Don't sit around and expect other people to do it for you.

So if a head hunter promised to call you or send you some information and you haven't heard anything when you expected to, give him or her a call or send an email as a reminder. They may simply have forgotten, impossible as that may seem to you.

Or let's say you have interviewed with a few places, but there is one company that you are really enthusiastic about. You were supposed to get feedback on Monday, but it's Wednesday and you haven't heard anything. Give them a call to see what is happening! Let the company know that you really, really want to work for them.

Another thing you can do is write a thank you letter to your interviewer.

Don't go overboard with the eagerness, however. You don't want to become a stalker. And if a company explicitly says that you should just wait until you hear from them, and not call, then respect their wishes. Use your judgement.

If you are a student interviewing companies that come on campus, there may be a predefined schedule that the companies stick to, and you may not be left wondering very long whether or not you have made it to the next round, or received a job offer. Nevertheless, there may still be times when a follow-up call or email could be useful. Again, use your judgement.

Just a note on thank you letters: there are many interview guides that state that thank you letters are a must - i.e. after every single interview you should send a note (or email) to your interviewers, thanking them for the meeting. Some people swear by this. However, I have never written general thank you notes because I don't think they will sway the outcome of the interview. And they can take up a lot of time during an intense period of interviewing – I would rather spend that time preparing for my next interview, practising my stock pitches, etc. That being said, as I mentioned above, a thank you letter can be used strategically to let a company know you are really interested.

Know When to Give Up

Unfortunately, there will come a time when the game is over and you have to give up on a company. You have pulled out all the stops, expressed your enthusiasm for the role, but to no avail. This point is usually reached when the company officially turns you down, i.e. lets you know either verbally or in writing that you are no longer being considered for the role. Alternatively, if you don't hear from a company for an extended period of time, despite your best efforts to make contact, you can assume that they are no longer interested (and also rather rude).

I would seriously advise that you give up once you have been rejected. Don't call the company up and beg them to reconsider. Don't write letters to the people you met, telling them what a mistake they made. You can ask for feedback, but don't try to change anyone's mind. Persistence is okay until you have been rejected, but not afterwards.

People usually have solid reasons why they have rejected a candidate. They may not always be the best reasons, but once a company has decided that a certain person is not suitable for them at a particular point in time, they are unlikely to change this opinion. Remember, these reasons could be things that you can't do anything about (maybe you just rubbed someone the wrong way, or maybe there was someone else who was exactly what they were looking for). You may never know exactly why you got turned down, so don't obsess too much about it.

Move on to the next opportunity. That would be my advice.

Interviewing is like Dating

I think that a good analogy for the interview process is dating. Yes, interviewing is like dating. If you think about it that way, it can help you to adapt the right attitude and philosophical approach.

At the end of the process, instead of a marriage proposal, you get a job offer (and the company has to make the job offer proposal, whether you are a man or a woman).

Before you get to that point, you and the company have to go on a series of interviews (dates). You dress up nicely, smile, and put on your best behaviour in order to impress. To some extent, they do the same. Then if you both like each other, you go on a bunch of other dates (interviews) to get to know each other better.

When you are on a date with someone you want to impress, you are enthusiastic, pleasant, and an overall nice person. You follow-up, call, and show your interest, but not to the point of being creepy or bordering on stalking. You don't act bored, cynical, or in an arrogant or rude fashion.

In addition, going on dates can and should be fun. You are learning about someone new and they are learning about you. It is a two-way street. Similarly, you should use your interviews to find out more about each company and figure out whether or not they are a good fit for you, and whether you would ultimately be happy working there.

If it all goes well, after a few interviews (dates), the company will propose, and then you can either accept or reject this (job) offer.

However, as anyone who has dated knows, it doesn't always go well. Sometimes you or the other person knows after the very first date that it is not going to work out. Sometimes you like the other person but they don't like you, or vice versa. Rejection is par for the course. Sometimes you can go out for quite a long time and almost, almost make it to the proposal stage. But then for some reason it all falls apart. This is what can happen when you are interviewing as well.

However, the good news is that if you are persistent, and willing to consider many of the possibilities out there, you are likely to eventually get a job.

Try to Get a Summer Job in Research

If you are a student, I would strongly advise you to try to get a summer job in equity research the year before you graduate (or in previous years). This will set you up well for your full-time job interviews. Companies that may have been sceptical about your interest in the industry are more likely to take you seriously if you have at least worked in research for the summer.

Obviously, it would be best if you could manage to get a buy-side equity research job if that is your ultimate aim. Most of the advice I have given in this book applies equally well to finding a summer job. If you do get a summer job, try to work really hard, impress the company, and get an offer for a full-time position at the end of the summer. Even if you know that you don't want to work for that particular company full-time, it is still good to have an offer in your pocket. At the very least, you can use it as leverage with other firms. Knowing that you have an offer from another company makes you instantly more desirable to others.

If you don't get a buy side job for the summer, then the next best option is a sell-side job. So do interview with them as well. And do try to get an offer at the end of the summer.

If you are not able to get a sell-side research summer job either, then try to work in an area where you are required to learn and display some of the same skills that are called upon in the equity analyst role: research, valuation, analysis, finance, interviewing others, and financial market knowledge. Some occupations that come to mind include management consulting and other areas of finance like private equity and venture capital. Note that some of these areas are just as hard, or even harder, to get into than the buy-side when you are a student. Investment banking, corporate finance, and sales & trading are also options.

Do Interview at Many Different Places

One decision you need to make is how focused your job search will be. Will you only apply to the buy side? Will you interview with the sell-side as well? Will you extend your search outside of research altogether, and look at investment banking or management consulting or marketing?

You need to make this decision for yourself, but at the very least, I think you should look at the sell side as well as the buy side. Getting an equity research position can be quite a competitive process, on both the buy and sell side. You should hedge yourself just in case you are not successful this time around.

Now when you do look at the buy side, you should cast quite a wide net, and try to interview at as many places as possible. Don't decide that you only want to work for Fidelity or Capital or for a certain hedge fund. The key is to break into the industry and get some experience. Later on, if you still choose to, you can try to apply to the firm of your dreams.

As I mentioned earlier in the book, almost any equity research experience will be looked upon as valuable to a potential employer. There are many buy side firms out there, even though they may not hire in the bulk that some sell-side firms do.

Remember, you may have to interview with 5, 10, or even 20 firms to get one offer, so apply to many places!

The dynamics of your situation and the job market should influence how you go about getting your interviews. If you are in business school or university and several firms come to your campus, you may choose to initially limit your interviewing to those companies. Then if you are not successful, you could be more active in searching other companies out (I discuss this process in some detail in Chapter 3). Alternatively, you may decide to cast a wider net from the start because you want to target more firms than just the ones that come to your school. It's up to you. For the record, both my summer and full-time jobs out of business school (both on the buy side) were with companies I applied to through the on campus recruitment process, and that's the only place I looked. I focused my interviewing on research and looked at both the buy and sell side. But I went to a large business school that most of the big asset management companies came to. If your situation is different, you may want to adjust your tactics.

As for the job market, if you are lucky enough to be graduating at a time of economic prosperity with a roaring bull market and plentiful jobs, then sticking with the companies that come on campus may be good enough; many are likely to come. If, however, you end up starting your job search during a recession or financial crisis, you are probably going to have to work a lot harder.

Don't be Late for Interviews... or Too Early

This is obvious, but I still feel the need to say it: don't be late for your interviews. Do whatever it takes to get there on time. If you have to travel a long distance, plan your trip in advance. Make room for contingencies like delayed buses, late trains, or traffic jams.

Why is this so important? Well, if you are late, the company you are interviewing with may take this as a sign of something deeper: that you are not good at planning, that you are nonchalant about the opportunity, or that you think being late for meetings is okay.

None of this may be true, you may just have been unlucky and missed your bus, but they won't know that.

Don't arrive exactly on the dot of the time at which you are supposed to interview either, arrive 5-10 minutes beforehand. If your interview is supposed to start at 4pm, you can't arrive at exactly 4pm because it will take at least 5 minutes for you to be greeted and settled. Also take into account the fact that some places may have security procedures where you will be required to sign in or even have your picture taken before you are given access to the building.

A somewhat less obvious point is that you should not be too early either. Being very early (20-30 minutes or more) for an interview is also a bit rude. This is because your interviewers are probably busy doing other things up until the point you have your interview. They may have other meetings or work scheduled. However, once you do show up, they will feel obliged to attend to you; no one likes the prospect of another person sitting and waiting for them in the lobby for half an hour.

If you do find yourself arriving extremely early, then try to find a nearby Starbucks or Prêt a Manger or the like, and wait there until a more appropriate time. If that is not possible, just walk around the area for a while.

Having said all of this - if you do find yourself arriving late - or if you are very early and cannot go anywhere else to make up the time, just make sure to apologize profusely when you do arrive.

Do Research on Each Company You Interview With

As I've mentioned in earlier sections of this book, it pays to do some research on each company you are going to interview with before you meet with it.

You can often get most of the information you need from the company's own website. Try to find out how large the company is (assets under management, employees, investment professionals), its investment style (value, core, growth, etc), geographic focus (e.g. US, Asian, global) and structure (career analysts, analyst/fund manager hybrid roles, etc). Also know whether it is long only or long/short.

The description of the job you are applying for often includes some background information of this type.

Please adjust your interview answers and even stock pick to the type of company you are interviewing with.

For instance, if you are interviewing with a firm that is looking to hire career analysts, i.e. people whose goal is to remain working as an analyst for a long time, then don't say that your primary goal is to become a fund manager. If it really is, and you won't be happy with anything else, then you probably should not bother interviewing with this company. If your plan is to work there for a few years and then leave to become a fund manager somewhere else, then yes, you can interview there, but that's obviously not something you would say to the company.

As another example, if a company has a value-driven investment style, don't go in with a high growth, high multiple stock. On the other hand, if you are interviewing with a growth manager, you might not want to pitch a really beaten up stock that is quite cheap but has no growth prospects. Because of this, it's best to come up with a stock pitch than sits nicely in the middle, as I mentioned in Chapter 4(II).

If you have the time, it can be useful to look up the types of stocks the company owns in its portfolios to give you a better idea of its investment style. If you have access to a service like Bloomberg, you can use that. If not, there are some free websites where you can access at least partial data. One example is **www.stockpickr.com**. In addition, most investment firms are required to file a 13F form every quarter with the SEC, which outlines the securities they hold. This applies to institutional investors with more than $100 million in assets under management and includes non-U.S. firms. However, only securities that are traded on U.S. exchanges will be listed (e.g. the New York Stock Exchange). See www.secinfo.com.

Holdings data will not be very useful for extremely large companies that have dozens of portfolios with varying investment styles. They are likely to own almost everything in one fund or another. But if you are meeting with a small, focused firm, the stocks it owns could shed some light on it.

Once You Get an Offer (Or You Are Close)

Hopefully that blessed day will come when all the preparation and hard work pay off, and you are offered a job. Congratulations!

Be Sure You Actually Have an Offer

First of all, don't count your chickens until they hatch. By this I mean don't assume you have an offer until you actually have one. A company may say things that sound like they are going to give you an offer. Examples include, "We really like you, and we are preparing to make you an offer"; "There is just one more step, a dinner with the CIO, after which you will get an offer, assuming that she doesn't object"; "You basically have an offer, but you have to take and pass a psychometric test first".

Anytime you are told that you have one more step before you get an offer, don't assume that you have it yet. Don't get blinded just because the word "offer" was used in the sentence.

You May Want to Continue Interviewing

In particular, if you are interviewing with other companies, please continue to do so. It can be tempting to end the tedious interviewing process with other firms, especially if you are close with one of your top choices. But that is not a good idea.

First of all, the offer may not come through in the end, or it may be unsatisfactory in some way. Second, it is good to have multiple offers if you possibly can. It gives you more leverage and negotiating power, or at least makes you seem more desirable to other companies. You can also use the offer at one firm to pressure another one to make a decision. You can let them know that you have a competing offer and that you need to either accept or reject it soon, so you need to know whether you are going to receive an offer from them as well.

For these reasons, even if you are very close to getting an offer from your top choice, or already have one, it makes sense to complete the process with other companies if you are at a similarly advanced stage with them as well.

Beware the Exploding Offer

Be aware that some companies will try to pressure you to accept an offer very quickly. This is to lock you in and prevent you from having the time to get competing offers from other firms. Sometimes you may be given an "exploding offer", i.e. one that will be retracted if you don't say yes in a very short period of time. This can be annoying and unfair, and some universities and business schools have policies against this for companies that recruit their students. Check whether your school does, and if so, let the company know that they are violating the school's rules. Of course, the company deserves to be told your answer in a reasonable amount of time, but pressuring you to make a decision in two days in the middle of interview season at your university is unacceptable, I think. Try to push back as much as you can, and get more time.

Once You Accept You Can't Retract

Note that it is considered very bad form to break your agreement once you accept a company's job offer. If you have told a firm that you will work for them, it will be looked upon very poorly if you later change your mind. In fact some universities and business schools may have policies against this and penalties for students who do it.

Companies Rarely Rescind Offers, but it Can Happen

Similarly, it is considered very bad for a company to break its promise to hire you. This is called rescinding an offer. Because of this, companies rarely do it. It does happen occasionally, however, for example during a severe economic or financial crisis.

Accept, Reject, or Negotiate

The upshot is this: consider your decision to accept an offer very carefully, because you won't be able to undo the decision.

In addition to accepting any offer you get, you can of course reject it. If you do reject an offer, be polite about it. And be prepared to give the company an explanation if they ask for it. But don't feel guilty. You have to make the decision that's right for you.

Another option is to negotiate the offer before you finally accept or reject it.

What Part of the Offer Can Be Negotiated?

Students should note that it is usually difficult for them to negotiate their job package because their offers tend to be standardized. It is very difficult for a firm to pay one student graduating from business school much more or less than another student graduating from business school (especially when it comes to the salary; your bonus will be determined by individual performance and may vary a lot more). Some more minor things might be negotiable, for example your start date.

Experienced, one-off hires are in a very different position. Then you can and should expect to negotiate.

Almost any aspect of an offer is open for negotiation: salary, bonus/bonus range, redundancy terms, notice period, title, benefits, etc. If you have competing offers, your position will be strengthened. I will admit here that negotiation is not one of my fortes, so I won't attempt to write much about it. If you are looking to do some serious haggling, you might want to consult some books or other resources on the topic. I have listed one in the Appendix.

Take Time to Investigate the Firm

If you are considering accepting an offer from one or more firms but you are unsure about whether or not you would be happy there, ask the firm to let you spend some more time with the company. You might want to go in and talk to people that you didn't meet during the interview process, or have lunch with your potential boss and/or colleagues. Some firms might even let you come in for a whole day and attend meetings, etc, so that you can get a real sense of what the environment is like. Remember, the companies want you to accept their job offer, so they are likely to be accommodative to a reasonable request. You may also want to do additional research on the company by speaking to former employees. Current employees may feel obliged to put a positive spin on things out of loyalty to their employer, but former workers are under no such constraints. They are much more likely to give you the real deal about a company's culture, practices, and people, as well as the specifics of the job you are thinking of taking: duties, hours, compensation, and career progression.

Get the Offer in Writing

Finally, make sure that you do get the offer in writing, and read it carefully. Note that some companies will only send you the full document once you have accepted the offer and the major terms have been agreed verbally (like salary, start date, etc). If you are unhappy with anything in the offer, let the company know, and ask them to adjust it *before* you sign it. Once again, if it is a standard offer that they are giving out to all students at your level, there is likely to be little flexibility here. But don't be afraid to ask questions about something that you are unsure about.

Chapter 6

If You Don't Succeed This Time

This chapter is for you if, despite following the guidelines in this book and giving the interview process your best effort, you still have not succeeded in getting an equity research job offer.

Try to Find the Problem

First, try to find out what went wrong, and address the problem. If you failed to get interviews, there could be a problem with your resume/CV, and/or the way you are targeting firms. If you did succeed in getting interviews, but didn't progress very far, try to get feedback from the companies about what went wrong, and why you were not invited back. Ask them while they are still likely to remember you. Don't wait until 6 months have passed from the day you had your interview.

Realize that sometimes the problem may be that you were simply unlucky with your timing. A major recession or financial crisis can cause companies to sharply reduce or even halt their hiring. In fact, many companies start firing people, a rather common occurrence in the financial world, unfortunately. That means that, in addition to everything else, there will be lots of experienced people out of work who are competing with you for jobs. Demand for jobs will have increased at the same time that supply decreased. If you are graduating from business school or applying for jobs at a time like this, your chances of getting a job will be greatly reduced, through no fault of your own.

Give Up or Carry On?

After evaluating the reasons why you didn't succeed, you need to decide what you are going to do. There are two main options: you can give up on equity research and decide to do something else, or you can continue to pursue it. If you choose option 1 then our journey together ends for now.

If you have decided that you want to try again, then read on.

Work Somewhere Else then Reapply

My main advice is this: try to get a job in a related field and re-apply in a year or two. I think this is a better option than remaining unemployed, even voluntarily. Prospective employers tend to prefer to see that you have done something, as opposed to large gaps on your resume. Of course, if you decide that you want to take off and travel the world for a year, or do something else equally worthwhile, this doesn't apply. Otherwise, doing a job that builds up some of the skills you will need and use in equity research is a good idea.

Potential Alternative Jobs

Some of these jobs have been mentioned in other chapters. Note that getting some of them can be quite a competitive process as well.

They include:

Sell-Side Research: the sell-side analyst role is the one most directly comparable to the buy-side, and the easiest to switch from. I described the sell-side in Chapter 1.

Management Consulting: management consultants advise firms on various aspects of their business, from strategy to operations. When you enter as an analyst, your role typically involves research, analysis, interviewing, and presenting. Some of this experience is useful in equity research.

Venture Capital/Private Equity: venture capital and private equity firms differ from the asset management companies we have been talking about in that they invest in private companies, not ones that are trading on public market stock exchanges. Venture capitalists tend to invest in companies that are quite early in their development, or near the start-up phase. Private equity firms usually invest in more established companies, and often get involved in leverage buyouts (LBOs). As you can imagine, some of the skills that go into analyzing private companies can be easily transferred to publicly-traded ones.

Corporate Finance: this is often what people mean when they say they work in "investment banking". The corporate finance role involves advising companies as they raise capital (debt or equity) in the public markets, or if they want to do mergers and acquisitions (M&A). Analysts usually have to build and work with detailed financial models for companies, and this can be useful for equity research. There is also a certain amount of market awareness that will come with the job. However, there are some potentially less interesting aspects to the role as well, including the creation of "pitch books" for prospective clients. The corporate finance job is also notorious for its very long working hours. Note that many hedge funds seem to prefer hiring people that have worked in investment banking before, so if you are set on working at a hedge fund, this might be the right path for you.

Equity Sales: salespeople sit between the sell-side research analysts and their buy-side clients. They aggregate and sift through ideas, and present the information that they think will be the most useful to the buy-side. Some salespeople come up with investment ideas of their own. They have to be knowledgeable about companies, but usually not to the same depth as analysts. They are usually well in the flow of what drives the markets. The job involves a lot of calling and speaking to people, so interpersonal skills are very important.

Equity Trading/Dealing: traders (also called dealers) do the actual buying and selling of equities. They typically work within investment banks, often in the same division as equity sales. Traders typically work on behalf of their firm's clients, but if they trade for the bank itself, they are called proprietary traders. Trading is very execution-oriented, and, of the jobs described so far, is probably the furthest from equity research. Proprietary trading, where people come up with their own ideas to trade for the firm, is closer.

Other Investment Banking and Finance Jobs: there are various other front-office roles that can be found in investment banks, things like equity capital markets, wealth management, private banking, and principal investing. These could help you to build some useful skills as well. In addition, it is sometimes possible to move into equity research from support roles on the buy side such as fund accounting and client relationship management.

Consider Fixed Income

Note that you don't necessarily have to stick to equities, though that would of course be better if you eventually want to do equity research. But if you get a job doing fixed income research, for example, you could also make the switch to equities later on.

Other Jobs

If you don't get a job in one of these areas, all is still not lost. You can do something totally different like work in industry or marketing, and still try to make the transfer to research later on.

Don't Wait Too Long

My advice, however, would be not to wait too long. Try to move within 1-3 years. The longer you do something else, especially something completely different, the harder it will be for you to transfer to equity research. The sell-side is an exception, as it is quite easy to make the move between the two at almost any point in one's career. That being said, there may be a few asset management firms that prefer their experienced hires to have buy-side experience, so if you are really set on the buy-side, I would advise you to make the switch relatively soon.

Chapter 7

Now That You've Got the Job: A Few Tips

This chapter is for you if you have been successful in finding a buy side equity research job. If this book has helped you in any way, then my main mission has been accomplished.

Congratulations, by the way!

I thought I would add one more chapter to get you started on the right foot when you begin working.

The thing is - the role of an equity analyst involves a lot more than just picking stocks. That is the central job, of course. But in addition to that, you have to be good at putting your ideas in written form, presenting them to the portfolio managers, knowing what to do when stocks go wrong, understanding what drives the markets, working with the sell-side, dealing with company management teams and investor relations, and keeping your director of research happy, just to name a few things.

So I am going to share a few key tips with you. Many of them are things that I did *not* do when I first started out, and suffered because of it. I wish someone had told me then what I know now.

Please note that some of the advice I am giving below will make the most sense for people who have their own stocks that they are responsible for covering. Business school graduates and experienced hires are likely to be in this position. Students who have just graduated from university may be assigned to work with a more senior analyst when they first enter the industry, as I explained in an earlier chapter. Therefore some of the tips I give will be relevant to them but others will only make sense if, and when, they become the main analyst on a group of stocks.

Please note that I am going to use the terms "Fund Manager" and "Portfolio Manager" interchangeably.

Be Very Careful of What You Say to the Portfolio Managers

When you are an analyst, your dialogue with the portfolio managers (PMs) is very important. Your main role, after all, is to provide them with stock recommendations, i.e. whether they should buy, sell, or hold the stocks that you are responsible for covering in their portfolios.

You must therefore watch what you say to them very carefully. Don't blurt things out without thinking them through. Every word that you say is being judged. Don't forget that.

In particular, do not give a recommendation on a stock until you are sure about it. If you are pressed, you can say something non-committal like, "My initial view is slightly favourable, but I really need to do more work on the valuation before coming out with my recommendation".

You need to be especially careful when you first join a firm because initial impressions can last a very long time. Once you blow your reputation with the PMs, that's it – it's very hard to get it back.

You need to come across as intelligent, knowledgeable, and inquisitive. You need to radiate confidence about your ratings. At the same time, however, unless you are coming in as an experienced analyst, the fund managers know that you probably don't know much about the sector or stocks you have been assigned to cover when you first start, i.e. that you are just learning. So it is a somewhat tricky balance. You need to show that you have done a lot of work on your companies, and because of that, you do have some insight into the stocks you are presenting. Generally, your reputation as an analyst will slowly build up over time as you prove your stock-picking abilities. You need to aid this process by being very careful about what you say and present to the fund managers.

Manage Your Relationship with the Portfolio Managers

As I mentioned, your relationship with the fund managers is key. It can be the source of lots of conflict if it is not handled well.

First of all, you need to accept the fact that unless you are at a firm where the analysts also run the funds, a very large part of your job is supporting the PMs with their investment decisions. You can love or hate a particular stock, and try your best to convince the fund managers of your views, but at the end of the day, the decision is theirs as to whether or not it goes into or comes out of a fund. Some analysts struggle continually with this concept, and if you do you will always be unhappy. So either accept the fact that the fund manager has the final decision and make peace with it, or try to become a fund manager yourself so that you have the final say.

Note that sometimes a portfolio manager may like a stock idea of yours in principle, but is unable to put it into a fund because of portfolio construction reasons. The fund may already be too overweight in the sector, or maybe there are liquidity, size, or other constraints that make it impossible for the stock to be bought. Most fund managers will let you know why they are not buying one of your stocks if you ask.

The best type of relationship happens when you have built up a good reputation. The portfolio managers trust your recommendations, and because of that, they are willing to put most of your ideas into their funds, once you have argued your case well and presented them with the appropriate data. But it can take a while before that happens. Don't just wait for it, however. take an active role in building your professional relationship with the PMs.

If you are finding it difficult to communicate with a particular fund manager, make a special effort to reach him or her. Go to this person's office; ask questions about their investment style, the type of ideas that go into their portfolios, and how you can help. You'll be surprised how many analysts never do this sort of thing. Another approach you can take is to ask an analyst who seems to work well with this fund manager how he or she does it.

The portfolio managers will almost inevitably have some say in your performance review (which usually plays a part in the determination of your bonus). Don't wait until your review to find out what they think of you. See if you can get a sense of that beforehand. You may not be able to bluntly ask, "What do you think about me?", but you can try some more subtle questioning. The best way is if you have a constant dialogue, and you are often talking to the PMs about stocks and getting some of them into their portfolios. A good working relationship is the best way to set yourself up for a good review.

If you are in a firm with many different portfolio teams and portfolio managers, it may be the case that some of them are more crucial to your evaluation as an analyst than others. Try to determine which ones those are beforehand, and make sure you spend a lot of time building up your relationships with them. Don't ignore the others, but do put a lot of effort into the teams that have the greatest influence on your career.

Note that in many firms, your performance will be judged partly on the impact you had in the portfolios, not just on how well your stock recommendations have done. So even if you are the most brilliant analyst in the world, and all of your stocks perform the way you predicted, if you weren't able to convince any of the fund managers to put your ideas into their funds, you will generally be deemed, at best, only partly effective. You will get some credit, of course, but not as much as if your ideas actually had an impact. This is yet another reason to work on and manage your relationship with the portfolio managers.

Have Conviction

As I've mentioned before in this book, having conviction about your stock calls is key to being perceived as a good analyst. No portfolio manager is going to want to buy one of your stocks if you are lukewarm about it.

If you are unsure about a stock, then don't rate it as a buy. Leave it as a hold or a neutral.

Having conviction doesn't mean blindly loving a company or a stock no matter what. (Yes, people actually talk about "falling in love" with stocks in this business.) You need to acknowledge the risks associated with your ideas, other points of view on the company, and things that could potentially go wrong. But the point is, having taken all of that into account, you need to come down one way or the other: buy or sell.

Remember, the fund managers are going to put very large sums of money (sometimes in the millions) behind your stock recommendations. Their reputations are on the line as well, because they will be judged by how their portfolios perform, and a portfolio is made up of several stocks. So in order to get this level of commitment, you first have to show that you yourself believe in the stocks you are pitching. Be sure about your recommendations and enthusiastic about them.

That being said, if you genuinely don't know something about a company, you can admit it. Say "I actually don't know the answer to that, but I'll find out". And then go and find out, and come back with the answer.

Another way to think about this is that there is very little downside to having conviction on an idea. Whether you end up being right or wrong, having conviction is the winning hand to play.

What do I mean?

Well, let's suppose you put a buy recommendation on a stock. One of two things can happen: the stock can go up a lot, or outperform its benchmark, in which case you were right, or it can go down a lot, or underperform, in which case you were wrong. (Of course, the stock could also just not do much and stay around the same level, but let's simplify the case to the two choices above.)

Now let's say you presented the stock with a great deal of enthusiasm and conviction and a few fund managers bought it. If it does well, then everyone will remember that you championed the stock, and give you credit for getting it into their portfolios. If it does badly, everyone will remember that too. But people know that bad things happen sometimes, analysts (and fund managers) will get things wrong, and they will figure this was one of those times.

Now let's examine what would have happened if you presented the stock as a buy, but you were lukewarm about the idea, clearly lacking any real conviction. But the same few fund managers decided to buy it anyway. If the stock does well, you will get a bit of credit, but not nearly as much as if you had been really enthusiastic about it. Some fund managers might even decide that they bought it more because they liked it than because you pushed it. If the stock does badly however, you will not get much less of the blame than you would have if you had presented it with conviction. It's human nature to act like this. People will once again figure that you just got this one wrong.

So you see, you get additional credit for having conviction when you are right (because it is so clear that you were squarely behind the idea no one can claim it wasn't yours). But you don't get the equivalent amount of credit for *lacking* conviction when you are wrong - you are likely to get the same amount of blame either way.

So it pays to have conviction.

Admit When You Are Wrong

Picking stocks is not easy. There are tons of factors that can affect the markets and an individual stock's price in the short and long term: interest rates, economic data, earnings, money flow, investors' emotions like fear and greed, mergers & acquisitions, etc, etc.

Inevitably, at some point in your career, you are going to get a stock call wrong.

As an analyst, you need to recognize when you are wrong on a stock. Having conviction is good and necessary, but you also need to keep re-evaluating the data that you get about a company and/or its industry to see if the thesis behind why you bought it is still valid.

If something changes with the company and/or its stock price, your thesis may have to change. You may have to admit that you were wrong about the company.

An example might be that you recommended a stock because you strongly believed the company's margins were going to improve significantly over the next 6 months, and because of that you expected it to beat consensus earnings expectations. If the company reports declining margins instead, misses earnings, and the stock falls, you may need to admit that you were wrong, and sell the stock. Resist the urge to justify still owning it by changing your original thesis to suit the current facts. (On the other hand, if the stock has become ridiculously cheap, it might be worth hanging on to it for that reason. But my central point remains, about admitting being wrong in the first place.)

Most human beings don't like to admit defeat, but it is essential to be able to embrace this as an analyst. Otherwise you may end up, for example, holding on to your buy rating on a stock as it falls from $50 a share to $35 to $25 and even lower, mainly because you don't want to accept the possibility that you made a mistake buying it in the first place. This is disastrous.

Sometimes it makes sense to sell a stock for $25 that you bought for $50. If the stock is going to $10, selling it at $25 is the right thing to do, even if you feel like an idiot. You will feel even worse if you don't sell it and it goes to $10. Similarly, it may make sense to buy a stock at $50 that you previously sold at $25. If you realize that the stock could go to $100, then you should be able to admit that you made a mistake selling it at $25, and that it is still a bargain at $50.

Observe What Successful Analysts Do

When you get to your new employer, have a look around. It will soon become clear which of the analysts are well-regarded by fund managers and people in senior positions. These are the analysts that people think are "good" or "strong", that the fund managers listen to and follow. Pick one of these analysts, one that you particularly admire and want to model yourself on, observe him or her carefully, and adopt his or her habits.

Observe how she talks to and handles the fund managers. Listen to when she talks and when she shuts up and listens to others. Observe when she says, "I don't know" and when she decides to bluff an answer.

Read the research notes that he has written. Ask him if you can sit in on his meetings with companies and observe the questions he asks, and how he communicates with management teams.

Try to copy many of these techniques and behaviours as you do your own work.

Find a Mentor

I think it is very important to find a mentor when you just join a firm, especially if you are new to equity research. Simply put, your mentor will be someone who can guide and support you during your time at the company.

Your mentor should be someone who works at your company, who is senior to you but you do not report to. (If you report to the person you may feel awkward about asking stupid questions.) This person should have a genuine interest in helping you. He or she could be very senior or only a year or two above you. The key is that the person is experienced enough to give you advice. A senior analyst on your team who can observe you in action would be ideal. Or it might be a fund manager. Of course, you can have more than one mentor.

It may take you a bit of time to find a mentor because you essentially need to make friends with someone and develop enough of a rapport that he or she feels an interest in helping you. That being said - don't be afraid to be proactive. You don't need to actually go up to someone and say, "Will you be my mentor?" Hopefully it will come about more naturally than that. You might start by asking an experienced analyst's opinion about one of your notes or models. If you get the brush-off or the person seems too busy, try someone else.

Some companies formally assign you a mentor. If that happens take advantage of it. You may still find an additional mentor on your own, but do use the one you have been provided with.

If you are an undergrad who has been assigned to work with a senior analyst, that person is likely to naturally act as a mentor to you. In fact, he or she may be partly judged on how well you come along as an analyst and how much you seem to be learning. So do lean on this person for teaching, guidance, and support. You may still want to look for another mentor, however, especially if your assigned analyst has an input into your performance review (which is likely) or if you find that you don't naturally have a good connection with him or her.

Aim to get your mentor's feedback every step of the way. Show him or her your models and notes before you present them to the fund managers or your director of research, at least initially. Ask for feedback after you have presented to the fund managers about how well you did. See if your mentor can find out what people think of you and ways you can improve.

You don't want to over-burden your mentor, so try to ask advice about the really important things. The good news is that as time goes on, your knowledge will increase and you will need help with fewer things. It is probably during those crucial first few months that you will most need your mentor's help. That being said, once you have a mentor, the relationship can last for a long time. You may want to continue to seek out this person's advice at important junctures in your career.

Don't Blow-Up on Your First Recommendation

Your first few months as an analyst at a firm are key to establishing your reputation. Most important are the first few stock recommendations you make. They are your debut, so to speak.

Now, everyone knows that you are new and that you still have a lot to learn. No one will expect you to be as impressive as an analyst who has been doing the job for 10 years. Nevertheless, you want to make a good impression.

I think one of the worst things you can do is have a big blow-up on your first stock recommendation. This is especially true if you get some fund managers to buy it.

By "blow-up" I mean a stock that goes down in a big way (if it is a buy; obviously, it would be the opposite if it is a short).

Now, no one can predict the future, and of course you would not intentionally pick a stock that is going to go down a lot. But there are always some stocks that tend to be more volatile than others. Very small cap names, highly levered companies (i.e. with lots of debt), companies that have had recent big earnings misses, and companies with high betas are generally more risky (where risk is measured by volatility). It is also true that some of these situations are the ones where you are likely to make the most money if you are right: the higher the risk, the higher the potential reward, and vice versa. So some people will say that you should go for the kill right away, and come out with a bold idea that has more of a chance of making the fund managers some real money.

My advice, however, would be to play it safe initially. If possible, go with a good, solid company with a strong balance sheet, and a prudent management team that is unlikely to do anything stupid in the near-term. This type of stock is much less likely to blow-up on you.

Be careful initially, and especially with your first recommendation. Save the high risk stuff for when you have gained a bit of a reputation, and earned some trust with the portfolio managers. After you have had a few stocks do well and make them some money, the fund managers will start to think of you as a good analyst. If you then have a blow-up, they will just assume that you had a bit of bad luck. If you start off with a blow-up, however, then their first impression will be that you are not a good analyst. And that is a very hard hole to climb out of.

I am aware that you may have to initiate on a group of stocks together. For example, you may have been assigned the U.S. discount retailer sector, and have to come up with recommendations on four names at the same time: Family Dollar, Dollar Tree, Big Lots and Dollar General. Let's assume for this example that you have 2 buys, 1 hold and 1 sell. The same principle applies here: try to make sure that your buy recommendations are reasonably "safe".

Be Nice to the Sell Side

Some buy-side analysts and fund managers have a rather arrogant, negative attitude towards the sell-side. They look down on sell-side research because, rightly or wrongly, they consider it less impartial than their own. In addition, because the balance of power is usually with the buy-side in the relationship, as the sell-side depends on analysts and fund managers to vote for them, some on the buy-side feel that they don't have to treat the sell-side very well.

You may pick up some of this when you start your job. You may hear other analysts and fund managers speaking about the sell-side in a disparaging manner. Some may even be slightly rude to the analysts or the salespeople in meetings or on the phone.

In my opinion, this is a very silly thing to do. My advice to you, as a buy-side analyst, is to be nice to the sell-side. There are many reasons for this.

First of all, it pays to be as nice as you can in your dealings with others at all times. What goes around comes around, as they say. There is no upside to being rude, arrogant, or acting in an unpleasant manner towards others. So your default mode should always be "nice" in the workplace.

Beyond that, there are several practical reasons why you should maintain good relationships with sell-side analysts and salespeople.

Your sell-side analyst counterpart can help you to learn about your companies when you are just starting your job. In addition to reading their notes, conversations with experienced sell-side analysts can give you a lot of insight into management teams, company histories, industry trends, what moves the stocks, etc. Remember, the sell-side tends to cover a smaller number of stocks than the typical buy-side analyst, and so they get to know the companies in great detail.

What's interesting is that the relationships that you build with the sell-side can last longer than your relationship with any employer, especially if you continue to cover the same sector as you move firms. Let's suppose that you cover European Chemical companies at your first job. Then four years later you move to another asset management company, also to cover European Chemicals. It is very likely that you will be talking to the same set of sell-side analysts that you did previously. So it pays to invest in having a good relationship with them from the start.

That brings me to the next point: the sell-side can be very helpful during career transitions. If you lose your job or want to find a new one, sell-side analysts, and even more so the salespeople, can be instrumental in letting you know about the opportunities that are out there. This is because the salespeople have several buy side clients in addition to your firm. They are often among the first to know if an analyst or fund manager has left another company, because they are talking to them all the time. And their clients may ask them to recommend people that they know if a position opens up. Obviously, sell side analysts and salespeople are much more likely to recommend you if you have a good relationship with them. If you have been rude and unpleasant, there is little incentive to help you.

In general, remember that the sell-side is full of good, hardworking people, trying to do their jobs, just like you. And you never know; you may end up there one day.

Don't Burn Bridges

The buy-side community is surprisingly small in many ways. You might find yourself meeting the same people over and over again. An analyst that you worked with during your first job in Boston might turn up as a fund manager at a company you are interviewing with 10 years later in London. A portfolio manager that you worked with at one company might be the CIO of another firm in five years time, and in a position to either help or harm your chances of getting hired. You may find that your reputation precedes you, and that people you have never even heard of have formed an opinion of you because they discussed you with their good friend, who you used to work for 3 years ago.

The point is, try to do good work, make a good impression, and form allies wherever you work. Don't burn bridges with people. It could come back to haunt you later.

Be Ethical

Establish and maintain the highest ethical standards during your career as an analyst or fund manager. When you enter the industry, your employer will outline several rules that you have to observe about (not) insider trading, gift acceptance, your ability to trade in your personal account, and other issues. Be sure to follow these guidelines to the letter. But you should go even beyond that. If you are ever unsure about the rights or wrongs of a particular situation, play it safe. Sometimes your gut instinct will alert you to impropriety, even though you may not be actually breaking a formal rule. Let that well-known Wall Street Journal test apply: don't do anything that you would not be happy to have published on the front page of the Wall Street Journal (or the Financial Times, if that is more applicable to you).

This is not just about morality. Being ethical is also very good practical advice. I have seen the reputation of an entire institution severely damaged because of the actions of some of its employees that were found to be unethical, if not technically illegal. The consequences were very tangible: lost assets and profits, management turmoil, and high employee turnover, to name a few. Plus you only have to read the daily news to hear about bankers, hedge fund managers, analysts, traders and others being censured, sued, and even arrested for improper behaviour. You don't ever want to be one of them. As I mentioned in Chapter 1, remember that your role is an important one. You are an intermediary in the capital markets, and this carries a certain level of responsibility.

Manage Your Career

In addition to being a good worker-bee analyst, you should try to manage your overall career trajectory. Take some time now and then to assess where you are and where you want to go next. Do you want to switch sectors? Should you try to broaden your geographic area of coverage? Do you want to become a fund manager? Would you prefer the sell-side? Are you being underpaid in your current position?

Keep in mind that no one else is going to push things forward for you. You are in charge of your own career. You may get lucky, and someone may offer you a better position at your company or at another firm. But it is best not to assume that anything will be handed to you.

I think it is a good idea to get on the lists of head hunters so that they will give you a call when a position that might be relevant for you comes up. You might choose to interview for other jobs now and then, even if you don't plan to move. It's good to know what else is out there and what you are worth in the market. Generally, it is not a good idea to let your current employer know that you are interviewing elsewhere.

I am not trying to encourage disloyalty towards your employer. But note that loyalty is a two-way street, and you can be sure that the moment your company decides they no longer need you, they will let you go. So you have to look after your own interests; don't trust your employer to do that for you.

You should also look out for signs that your company is in trouble, or any other changes that might threaten your job. Assets under management (the amount of money your company is managing for others) are the life blood of an investment management company. If your employer suddenly starts losing assets rapidly, beware. Also keep track of performance: if your company suffers major underperformance in some of its key funds, this could cause people to withdraw their money. If your funds are rated by consultants or agencies like Morningstar or Mercer, and they downgrade the rating, that could spell trouble as well. Also be watchful if your company is bought, taken over, merged with someone else, or if new management is brought in. Big changes like this can often be the precursor to changes in personnel, downsizing, or restructuring. If you sense that your job is under threat, start looking around for a new one, just in case.

Notes on Becoming a Fund Manager

As of the time of this book's writing, I have never been a portfolio manager. I have always been an analyst. So I can only tell you what I have observed about the transition from analyst to fund manager.

You should be aware that in some firms it is very difficult, if not impossible, to make this transition. It could be because the company only hires career analysts, or because there are too many people ahead of you in the queue to become fund managers, and there are very few positions available. If you are set on becoming a fund manager, try to find this information out. It may turn out that you will have to move to another company to follow your dream. If that is the case, you need to know.

On the other extreme, there are some companies where most analysts are expected to eventually become portfolio managers, and there is a defined career path. The ones who are not successful may be expected to leave. If so then make sure to speak to a few people who made the transition, to find out what made them successful.

Some companies may have a hybrid analyst/fund manager role. In others, you may come in explicitly as a trainee fund manager and work your way up.

At other companies it may be less explicit. There is a possibility of making the transition, but it is on a very case-by-case basis. In this situation, it is probably a good idea to make your wishes known to the management of your company, so that if an opportunity does arise they will know you are interested. In addition, it is good to implement a pull strategy as well as a push one, i.e. to try to get the fund managers to request that you join them. For example, if you decide that there is a particular portfolio group at your company that you would like to join one day, make an extra effort to get to know the fund managers on the team, and to bring them good ideas. Build up a good relationship with them. That way if they decide they want to bring a new person onto the team, they might approach you.

The key is to try to find out your possible career paths before you join the company. Then if you know that you want to become a fund manager some day you should set your plan in motion from the beginning.

What to Do if You Lose Your Job

Unfortunately, the world of finance is a volatile one, and there is always a risk that you may lose your job at some point. There is just not a lot of job security in this industry (or in almost any industry these days, for that matter). On that note, though it is somewhat beyond the scope of this book, I can't help but dispense the following advice: save some pennies for a rainy day. You never know when you might suddenly lose your job and have to live off your savings for a few months. Don't spend all your bonuses!

In the "Manage Your Career" section of this chapter, I advised you to keep a lookout for some signs that your company might be in trouble and/or your job might be at risk, so that you could take pre-emptive action. If you do lose your job before you have found something else, however, the first thing to realize is that it is not the end of the world. These things happen, I know from firsthand experience. Don't get into a panic.

As soon as you are ready, get back out there and start interviewing again. Be positive and confident. You may want to re-read some of the earlier chapters in this book which deal with how to get interviews, depending on your particular situation.

Make sure to have an answer when head hunters or potential employers ask why you are no longer working for your former employer. Have a brief explanation with the most positive angle that you can give it, and stick to your story everywhere you go. Don't lie, it is very likely to come back to haunt you. Word travels in this industry, and as I mentioned, it is quite a small world. Don't say you resigned if you were actually made redundant.

Try to use this time as an opportunity to really think about what you want to do next and advance your career. Maybe you will look over your CV and realize that you need to broaden your geographic coverage area, or that you'd like to change sectors. Or you might decide that now is the time to try to switch to a fund management position. Or you may decide to move from Boston to London.

Obviously, if you are running out of money or need to get a job as soon as possible for other reasons, you should just try to get something reasonable as quickly as you can. The easiest position for you to get will be one that is exactly like the one you held previously, perhaps at a more senior level. So if you were an analyst covering Japanese Transportation companies, it will be easy for another company to hire you to cover the same group, sector, or geography. You might have to do more convincing, as well as fend off more experienced competition, if you suddenly decide that you want to start covering U.S. Financials. That being said, it is possible to switch sectors and geographies completely, especially early in your career.

Remember that the sell-side can be a good alternative to the buy side for some people.

Don't Become Too Stressed

There are times when the life of an equity analyst can become very stressful. In particular, it can be very painful if a stock recommendation goes against you. For example, you do a ton of work on a company, become convinced that it is a strong buy with 40%+ upside, and get a bunch of fund managers to buy it. 2 weeks later the company reports disappointing earnings, and the stock falls 15% on the day. The fund managers are not happy and want to know whether they should sell it, do nothing, or buy more. You need to figure that out pronto. This is a stressful situation. You worry about what to do, and even whether you are in danger of losing your job.

The first thing you need to realize is that this sort of thing is bound to happen to you at one point or another. Almost every analyst out there is going to have a few blow-ups in his or her career. It is not the end of the world. In fact, you can view it as a sort of rite of passage. As I mentioned earlier in this chapter, try to make sure your first few recommendations don't blow up. But it is almost guaranteed that something like this will happen at some point. The fund managers know this too. Most fund managers started out as analysts, and they will have made their fair share of mistakes in both roles. So though they may be upset when you make a bad stock recommendation, you should realize that they will not be overly shocked. They know that these things happen to even the best analyst in the world. They *will* get over it.

Realistically, if you have a series of consistently bad stock calls over a sustained period of time, you might be asked to leave, or the portfolio managers might stop listening to your recommendations, which is almost as bad. But the odd blow-up here or there is not going to get you fired. (The exception might be at some hedge funds where, I have been told, their time frame for evaluating people is very short.)

As for yourself, try to keep some perspective. We all care about our careers, but it is just a job, at the end of the day. No job is worth sacrificing your health or sanity for. If you find that happening then take a step back and find a way to re-focus and reduce your level of stress.

Have Fun!

Equity research is a fascinating profession. You get to learn about companies and how they work. You often deal with management at the highest levels of the company: CEO, CFO, and other senior positions. If you actually went to work at those companies right out of university or business school, you would probably be several levels down from them.

You have to understand the strategies, financials, products, growth plans and anything else there is to know about different types of companies. You have to try to figure out what they are worth.

You often get to travel to interesting (and sometimes not so interesting) places to meet companies, talk to management, visit their factories, and observe their products.

You are at the epicentre of the financial world. Your recommendations can cause very large sums of money to be invested in the stock market. You are constantly pitting your intelligence against those of other market participants, who have different views from you about the worth of a particular security.

You attend conferences and learn about new developments in your industries of coverage.

You also get to work with and learn from very knowledgeable and often very sharp people: other analysts at your firm, fund managers, sell-side analysts, salespeople, and company management teams.

For someone who is interested in finance and the markets, this is stimulating, interesting, and exciting work. So make sure to remember to have fun with the job!

I wish you all the best in your career as an equity research analyst.

Appendix

I have listed here some additional resources that may help you during your job search or serve to increase your knowledge of finance, company analysis, the markets, and investing.

The website associated with this book is **www.dennyellison.com**. *Please visit it for additional information and updates.*

Financial Analysis, Accounting, and Valuation

Analysis for Financial Management, Robert C. Higgins

Business Analysis and Valuation: Using Financial Statements, Krishna G. Palepu and Paul M. Healy

Financial Shenanigans: How to Detect Accounting Gimmicks and Fraud in Financial Reports, Howard Schilit

How to Read a Financial Report: Wringing Vital Signs Out of the Numbers, John A. Tracy

Corporate Strategy

Competitive Strategy: Techniques for Analyzing Industries and Competitors, Michael E. Porter
Describes the famous "Porter's Five Forces"

CV/Resume Writing

The CV Book: Your Definitive Guide to Writing the Perfect CV, James Innes

The Resume.com Guide to Writing Unbeatable Resumes, Rose Curtis and Warren Simons

Interview Advice

Sell Yourself in Any Interview: Use Proven Sales Techniques to Land Your Dream Job, Oscar Adler

The Fast Track: The Insider's Guide to Winning Jobs in Management Consulting, Investment Banking and Securities Trading, Mariam Naficy

This book does not focus on research roles; however, a lot of the advice on resumes, cover letters, and general interview techniques is very applicable

Getting a Job in Hedge Funds: An Inside Look at How Funds Hire (A Glocap Guide), Adam Zoia with Aaron Finkel

Written by a search firm, Glocap, it gives case studies of people who have succeeded in getting jobs at hedge funds, and outlines typical entry paths

Value Investing

Getting Started in Value Investing, Charles S. Mizrahi

Value Investing, From Graham to Buffett and Beyond, Bruce C.N. Greenwald, Judd Kahn, Paul D. Sonkin and Michael van Biema

The Intelligent Investor, Benjamin Graham

Security Analysis, Benjamin Graham and David L. Dodd

Growth Investing

Common Stocks and Uncommon Profits and Other Writings, Philip A. Fisher

Stock Picking and Investing

One Up On Wall Street: How To Use What You Already Know To Make Money In The Market, Peter Lynch

Beating the Street, Peter Lynch

A Random Walk Down Wall Street, Burton G. Malkiel

Behavioural Finance

Behavioural Finance: Insights into Irrational Minds and Markets, James Montier

Extraordinary Popular Delusions and the Madness of Crowds, Charles Mackay

Negotiation

Get Paid What You're Worth: The Expert Negotiators' Guide to Salary and Compensation, Robin L. Pinkley and Gregory B. Northcraft

Tales of Finance: Classics, Modern Classics, and New Releases

To understand, be appalled by, or laugh at the world of finance and some of its key players, past and present

Liar's Poker, Michael Lewis

Den of Thieves, James B. Stewart

Barbarians at the Gate: The Fall of RJR Nabisco, Bryan Burrough and John Heylar

The Predators' Ball: The Inside Story of Drexel Burnham and the Rise of the Junk Bond Raiders, Connie Bruck

When Genius Failed: The Rise and Fall of Long-Term Capital Management, Roger Lowenstein

House of Cards: How Wall Street's Gamblers Broke Capitalism, William D. Cohan

The Devil's Casino: Friendship, Betrayal, and the High Stakes Games Played Inside Lehman Brothers, Vicky Ward

Too Big to Fail: Inside the Battle to Save Wall Street, Andrew Ross Sorkin

The Big Short: Inside the Doomsday Machine, Michael Lewis

Financial and Business Press

The Wall Street Journal

The Financial Times

Fortune

Bloomberg Business Week

Financial TV Channels

CNBC

Bloomberg Television

Financial Websites

For stock information - prices, earnings, analyst ratings, etc - as well as general financial news

Finance.yahoo.com

Finance.yahoo.co.uk

Finance.google.com

Finance.google.co.uk

www.multpl.com

Ycharts.com

Marketwatch.com

Stockpickr.com

Seekingalpha.com

123jump.com

Bloomberg.com

FT.com

WSJ.com

Paper Portfolios

Wallstreetsurvivor.com

Bullbarings.co.uk

Job Websites

efinancialcareers.com

efinancialcareers.co.uk

Major Search Firms aka Head Hunters, U.S. and UK

Please note that this is a selection, not a complete list

Russell Reynolds

Spencer Stuart

Heidrick & Struggles

Korn/Ferry

Odgers Berndtson

Whitney Group

Michael Page

Major Sell Side Firms

Please note that this is a selection, not a complete list

Morgan Stanley

Citi

Merrill Lynch (Bank of America)

J.P. Morgan

Goldman Sachs

Sanford Bernstein

Barclays Capital

UBS

Deutsche Bank

Credit Suisse

Major Buy Side Firms, U.S. and UK

Please note that this is a selection, not a complete list

Fidelity Investments

Capital Group

Wellington Management

MFS Investment Management

Putnam Investments

T. Rowe Price

Franklin Templeton Investments

Janus Capital Group

Pioneer Investments

Goldman Sachs Asset Management

J.P. Morgan Asset Management

UBS Global Asset Management

BlackRock

AllianceBernstein

Jupiter Asset Management

Schroders Investment Management

Newton Investment Management

Insight Investment Management

Threadneedle

Henderson Global Investors

M&G Investments

Brevan Howard Asset Management

GLG Partners

Och-Ziff Capital Management Group

SAC Capital

Citadel Asset Management

Made in the USA
Middletown, DE
21 January 2016